"I still have a page that goes into the Scotties' program every year and it's simply called 'Colleen by the Numbers.' It's virtually all the numbers and records that she established during her career. There are records she holds that will never be equaled, without question. The whole aspect of her longevity and her tenacity is remarkable. So for her to do what she's done for that period of time is amazing. I don't understand how she was able to do it, but it's a different person who can stay in the thick of things for that period of time and do well."

—Warren Hansen, director of event operations for the Canadian Curling Association

"They had something that no other team had. They were magic and it worked. They were teammates and incredibly good friends as well. They did things in the off-season together. I really think it comes down to Colleen and her role—she could make shots—and the karma and synergy that they had as individuals. You could see it. You couldn't deny it."

—Robin Wilson, coordinator of the Scotties Tournament of Hearts

"Colleen had a great ability to create a lot by her own self-confidence, being able to move from one area of expertise to another. She was also one of those who was willing to try just about anything in her career to see where it might take her and see what she might learn from it."

—Chuck Bridges, former director of news and information programming at CJCH and C100

"In 1988 she would have been one of the few [women sportscasters] working for us in Seoul, but she would have been one of the principal ones. Colleen's enthusiasm was one of her strengths. She was a contributor to the network for a long time and her talent got her to where she was. I grew up in Nova Scotia and I can speak to what it meant to people there to have her represent them on the national stage. There was a Nova Scotia Tourism spot that aired everywhere across the country, extolling all the virtues of the province—it ended with 'and the home of our Colleen.' Watching it, I remember thinking, 'Wow, they love her,' and as a Nova Scotian I knew why."

—Scott Oake, CBC broadcaster

"I could tell when Colleen got that feeling of winning versus not and therefore I just climbed on board. How could I tell? I spent every waking hour with her as her roommate. It was just the way she held herself. It was a level of calm. When she was comfortable, I was comfortable."

—Kim Kelly, teammate

"Colleen was not only hard on herself, but committed to being the best. She had the drive to be the best in the world, so sometimes that played out as being hard on herself. Other times it was her searching for a solution that may help her become a little bit better. In the curling world, I don't think they understood her because she was so driven. People took that as being arrogant, maybe non-friendly, but our relationship was always great. I know her fun side and other people wouldn't see that. They'd see her in a competitive mode when it wasn't the time to socialize."

—Ken Bagnell, team coach and mental trainer

"She provided a new territory as far as curling goes in being very visible and not being afraid to show her own personality. It's part of television. The world has changed and with that the persona of athletes themselves. The Scotties Tournament of Hearts gave them far more visibility than they'd had before, and Colleen was the perfect example of how to positively take that opportunity and inject her personality and enthusiasm in a way that brought great credit to herself, the sport of curling, and to women's curling."

—Bob Stewart, former chairman and CEO of Scott Paper Limited

"Her way of playing the game was always dismissed. She stubbornly stuck with it because she understood strategy isn't always about being just aggressive, it's about finding the best way to use the talent and the abilities you have amassed with your team to the best of your advantage. She understood how to do that in spite of all the rhetoric that was telling her 'you can't play this way. This isn't the way the modern game is played.'"

—Scott Saunders, Colleen's husband

"As a curler, she seemed like a force to be reckoned with. She was intense, sometimes unrecognizably intense because she was very loving and compassionate as a mother."

—Zach, Colleen's son

"When she was winning those Canadian championships she had brain fluid going into her lungs. She was winning Canadian championships on three hours of sleep, thinking she was sick and being short of breath—it's the untold story of how she won those championships."

—Luke, Colleen's son

THROWING ROCKS AT HOUSES

MY LIFE IN AND OUT OF CURLING

COLLEEN JONES
WITH PERRY LEFKO

VIKING

VIKING

an imprint of Penguin Canada Books Inc., a Penguin Random House Company

Published by the Penguin Group
Penguin Canada Books Inc., 320 Front Street West, Suite 1400, Toronto, Ontario
M5V 3B6, Canada

Penguin Group (USA) LLC, 375 Hudson Street, New York, New York 10014, U.S.A.
Penguin Books Ltd, 80 Strand, London WC2R 0RL, England
Penguin Ireland, 25 St Stephen's Green, Dublin 2, Ireland
(a division of Penguin Books Ltd)
Penguin Group (Australia), 707 Collins Street, Melbourne, Victoria 3008, Australia
(a division of Pearson Australia Group Pty Ltd)
Penguin Books India Pvt Ltd, 11 Community Centre, Panchsheel Park,
New Delhi – 110 017, India
Penguin Group (NZ), 67 Apollo Drive, Rosedale, Auckland 0632, New Zealand
(a division of Pearson New Zealand Ltd)
Penguin Books (South Africa) (Pty) Ltd, 24 Sturdee Avenue, Rosebank,
Johannesburg 2196, South Africa

Penguin Books Ltd, Registered Offices: 80 Strand, London WC2R 0RL, England

First published 2015

1 2 3 4 5 6 7 8 9 10   (RRD)

Manufactured in the U.S.A.

LIBRARY AND ARCHIVES CANADA CATALOGUING IN PUBLICATION

Jones, Colleen, 1959-, author
Throwing rocks at houses : my life in and out of curling / Colleen
Jones with Perry Lefko.

Includes index.
ISBN 978-0-670-06819-7 (bound)

1. Jones, Colleen, 1959-. 2. Curlers (Athletes)—Canada—Biography.
3. Broadcasters—Canada—Biography. 4. Curling. 5. Broadcasting.
I. Lefko, Perry, author II. Title.

GV845.62.J65A3 2015   796.964092   C2015-902934-1

Visit the Penguin Canada website at **www.penguin.ca**

Special and corporate bulk purchase rates available;
please see **www.penguin.ca/corporatesales** or call 1-800-810-3104.

To my boys: Scott, Zach & Luke; my best life teachers
—Carpe Diem

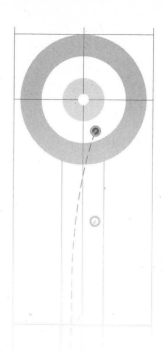

CONTENTS

Prologue 1

Chapter 1: The Meaning of Life 3
Chapter 2: Growing Up in Halifax 17
Chapter 3: The Game 35
Chapter 4: A Fresh Start 61
Chapter 5: Off the Ice 85
Chapter 6: Building Blocks 105
Chapter 7: The Championship Run 127
Chapter 8: All Good Things... 153
Chapter 9: Telling Stories 171
Chapter 10: Getting Back in the Game 193
Chapter 11: Zach and Luke 215
Chapter 12: The Circle of Life 225
Epilogue 235

Colleen by the Numbers 238
Afterword 239
Acknowledgments 242
Index 245

PROLOGUE

It's ironic that while I love telling other people's stories as a reporter, it was only when I sat down to start writing this book that I realized I have a hard time telling my own story. For some reason, everything I've done seems like nothing special.

Maybe it's my upbringing—stay humble—or maybe it's the sport of curling, which makes you even more humble. I don't think any curler looks at himself or herself as a star. You can be on top one day and losing the next. It's just the nature of the sport.

What I do know is I have stumbled on a lot of good fortune. I have worked really hard, and I've had to have a lot of discipline. But I've always marvelled at a few things: the good luck I've had along the way and the many people who gave me a helping hand and mentored me. I've been blessed. I've often felt I've had plenty of divine intervention in my life. Do I have a guardian angel looking out for me? I have no idea.

But I do have a wonderful family, a second family of fabulous curling teammates, and a third family at the CBC. Everyone's given me lots of chances and lots of help. I've always felt that I divide my life into three compartments: mother, curler, and worker. These have been three totally different roles. When I'm in "mom" mode, the nurturer and protector comes out. The person I am on the curling ice never shows up anywhere else. That is the intense part of my personality—very driven, very detail oriented. And when I'm working as a reporter, I'm in curious mode. I don't tend to mix all three of these roles because it would confuse everyone, including me.

So, after a lifetime of telling other people's stories, this is my story—about curling, broadcasting, growing up in Halifax in a family of nine siblings, marrying, starting my own family, surviving a serious health scare, and learning the hard way to savour life each and every day.

My long-time teammate and friend Nancy Delahunt always said about our curling team that "we really did just fall off the turnip truck." It seemed that every good thing that happened in our curling career just fell into place for us. Other teams were slicker and maybe even had more talent, but we had a chemistry and work ethic that pushed us to greater heights than we ever expected. I have six Canadian championships and two World titles. Not bad for a team that fell off the turnip truck.

CHAPTER 1
THE MEANING OF LIFE

It's funny how life is. I was starting to feel like I was sleep-walking through life a bit. We all have a rhythm to our lives—we wake up, brush our teeth, walk the dog, drink coffee, and get ourselves to work. Within this rhythm I was forgetting to enjoy the little moments—the proverbial "stop and smell the roses" part. I worried about silly things, like losing a curling game or being cut off in traffic. I was often lost in the past and busy planning the future.

Lucky for me, that sleepwalking didn't last forever. It often takes a huge event to wake us back up. Something happens that dramatically shifts our way of thinking and brings the realization that life is fragile. We are nothing without our health. It doesn't matter who you are or what you do. We are human beings who matter to the people we love and the people who love us, and it can all come to a sudden stop. Faced with this, it's then that we remember what is truly important and realize that it can be taken away in a moment. I learned this on December 10, 2010. On that day my life changed forever. Very fortunately, it changed for the better, because it was the day that I almost died.

It happened on a Saturday afternoon in Halifax. My husband, Scott, and I went to the farmers market to shop. I felt fine. We ate some food, bought a few things, and on the way home the world started to sway just a little bit. But I brushed it aside, and after we got home I left for my son Luke's junior curling practice. Luke was actually away at a tennis tournament in Florida, but I was coaching him and his friends. I was on the ice, setting up for a drill, when it hit me: nausea and dizziness. There was a pounding ache in the back of my head. I felt really sick and had to leave the club quickly. I climbed into my van, still wearing my curling shoes, and began to feel increasingly weak. Then I started throwing up. I live only five minutes from the club, but it felt like the longest drive of my life. I kept thinking, *What is going on?* It was just such a weird, surreal feeling, almost out of body. Of course I've had the flu before, but I had never felt anything like this. I really had no idea what was wrong, but I strongly wanted to get home and rest.

At home, I went into the nearest bedroom and curled up in the fetal position, wondering what was happening. Scott was home and came into the bedroom. He asked me what was wrong and I remember mumbling, "I don't know, but I think it's bad." Then I told him to call the 811 number we kept hearing advertised on the radio. In Nova Scotia, a new system had just started—people were supposed to call 811 to see if their medical problems really required a visit to the hospital. Scott described my symptoms and the person on the other end of the line dispatched an ambulance immediately.

I had a kind of floating feeling in which I was aware but not aware. The paramedics placed me on the stretcher and into the ambulance. All the while, I was telling them this was probably much ado about nothing—maybe a case of food poisoning—but I was drifting into limbo. They didn't sound the sirens, so that made me feel as though it wasn't serious. I started feeling nauseated and threw up again, and kept apologizing to the ambulance attendants. I couldn't shake the feeling that things were going downhill quickly. As this thought kept repeating in my mind, I got scared.

It all came out of the blue. One moment I was a healthy woman, doing something I loved, and the next I was in the fetal position. And it happened within about an hour. It turned out to be the most important hour of my life. I'm used to my body slip-sliding on the ice, but the feeling that my brain was slip-sliding was totally foreign to me. Everything had turned upside down.

Fortunately, we live close to the hospital. As I was being wheeled in I saw Doctor Petrie, who used to coach his son Sam and my son Luke on their basketball team. I waved to him feebly from the ambulance stretcher. Then things started slipping away, almost to the point where I lost consciousness. I was being poked with needles and having IV bags hooked up, and the medical staff was murmuring and whispering. Then I heard two words: *bacterial meningitis.* I actually bolted upright, panicked.

I knew the significance of what they were saying because I'm zany when it comes to reading articles on health. I knew that bacterial meningitis was one of those things that can be misdiagnosed as the flu or food poisoning. And it can kill you. Amazingly, just days earlier at the hospital, the emergency staff had been trained to identify symptoms of bacterial meningitis. They were working on improving the procedures for expediting people through emergency and recognizing what issues required immediate attention. In terms of high priority and serious concern, bacterial meningitis fit into the same category as stroke, heart attack, and trauma from a gunshot or car accident.

But I didn't know any of this then. All I knew was that the intuitive feeling in my gut that everything was going wrong now had a very serious and deadly name. I still couldn't believe any of this was happening. I had been scared before, but it was at this moment that I began to fear for my life. The thought of dying, there on a gurney in the emergency room, definitely crossed my mind and I had no control over whatever had been going on in my brain. I knew time was of the essence. I felt like I was standing beside myself, watching myself. I was trying to process what was going on and at the same time had probably lapsed into a mental fog because the drugs they'd given me had started to take effect. But the words *bacterial meningitis* snapped me into alertness. I knew there were possible complications such as brain damage, hearing loss, and learning disabilities. When it is caught in time, people can recover from bacterial meningitis, but it can also kill quickly.

Scott and our eldest son, Zach, were with me in the emergency room. They didn't know anything about bacterial meningitis at the time. Later, Zach told me he figured that anything that had "itis" in it couldn't be serious—like laryngitis and gingivitis. But within minutes both of them were on their phones doing a Google search on bacterial meningitis, learning how dangerous it was.

There are several types of germs (or pathogens) that can cause bacterial meningitis. In a nutshell, it causes inflammation in the lining of the brain and spinal cord, two places you really don't want that. Fortunately, it's not a common disease and the germs are not transmitted from one person to the next as easily as those that cause the flu or a cold. Also, the bacteria are not spread through simple contact or by breathing the air near a person who has meningitis. People can even carry the bacteria in their nose or throat without getting sick. Only rarely do these bacteria invade the body and cause illness. There are certain factors that make it easier for the disease to take hold in someone, and it turns out I had one of those.

While Scott and Zach were with me at the hospital, Luke was in Florida at a tennis tournament. We kept it quiet from him, but not deliberately—we were just focusing on the here and now. The urgency of the situation was taking all of our attention. I was in a pseudo quarantine. They hadn't confirmed yet what was wrong with me, and there was concern that I might have something infectious. So Scott and Zach sometimes had to wear full gowns and masks to enter the room to see me.

The doctors wanted to do a spinal tap, because it is the only way to tell for sure if a person has bacterial meningitis. Scott didn't want me to have the procedure because it can be risky. He remembered me having an epidural for Zach's birth and did not want another big needle inserted into my spine. I hadn't had any complications from the epidural, but needles in the spine come with risks. However, I was alert enough to shout "Just Do It," like the famous Nike ad, knowing the procedure was necessary. Within an hour, the sample came back positive, which was actually a huge relief because now we all knew what we were dealing with. If you've ever watched a TV medical drama like *House* or *Grey's Anatomy*, you know that a proper diagnosis is half the battle. Once the doctors were positive what was wrong, they could start treating me.

I remembered the feeling of helplessness when the slip-sliding had begun just hours earlier. With antibiotics and the magical steroid they gave me to reduce the brain's swelling, I began to feel almost hopeful, thinking that everything had been done and now it was just a matter of waiting it out. Perhaps I had started to accept what was happening, and some of the shock was wearing off. Not exactly a "que sera, sera; whatever will be, will be" moment, but I relaxed and felt no more panic. I think I just put my trust in God. I wasn't specifically praying for my health at that time, but I've always been a very spiritual person, always been very trusting that there's a path of some sort laid out for me. I had always had a good conversation with whatever is going on "up there," and I did feel that somebody was protecting me.

So, in a way, I was able to let go; I fully trusted that I was going to come through this. I let go of any anxiety, fear, and doubt and trusted. It's funny to me now, as this is exactly what I was trained to do in curling. Zach was massaging my head and hand and I felt surrounded by love. And then, at some point, I woke up. It felt so amazing. There had been a possibility that I wouldn't. I was surrounded by my medical team, including the internal medicine specialist, the infectious disease doctor, and a neurologist, and in almost a celebratory way they said to me, "You made it!"

Bacterial meningitis cases aren't everyday medical issues. The internal medicine specialist asked me how I thought the bug got into my brain. "What was the portal?" he asked. I told him that I had always joked with my curling teammates that I leaked brain fluid. For many years, a clear liquid dripped from my nose every time I put my head down, whether it was while doing yoga, cleaning the bathtub, or sweeping while curling. It wasn't like post-nasal drip, although that's what I thought it was the first time it happened. Years earlier I had even gone to my doctor thinking I had a sinus infection. It was treated with the usual antibiotics, but that didn't help. I thought it was just one of those quirky things I would always live with. Now it is obvious that I should have followed up with my doctor, but I came from "shake it off" parents. And I had always been a healthy person. I really just felt like someone with constant allergies.

When I told the doctor some of this, he asked, totally surprised, "Do you think you have a cerebral spinal fluid leak?" I wasn't even sure what that meant, and it was the last thing anyone would think, but that's exactly what had been going on during the height of my curling career in the early 2000s. The problem had even been affecting my sleep—every time I lay down, the fluid leaked into my throat, my lungs felt like what I imagine a smoker's feel like, and I'd wake up throughout the night, coughing and spitting up fluid. At the time, though, it just didn't seem very serious. Hindsight is a beautiful thing, and I can't believe I ignored all of the warning signs my body was giving me. But I had a daily to-do list to accomplish: Be a supermom, go to work and be a super-worker, and go compete and be a super-curler. Who had time to go see a doctor?

Before the "incident" I was thinking it had something to do with allergies. I would take over-the-counter allergy pills, but nothing stopped the flow. Wondering if my joke about a brain fluid leak had any truth to it, I actually tried to Google that possibility sometime in 2003. But nothing helpful came up. Now if I Google brain fluid leak, there is information. Days before I was hit with the bacterial meningitis, I was Googling my health issues and had convinced myself I might have pleurisy! Things had been getting worse—I was experiencing a steady drip of fluid—so I was planning to phone my doctor on Monday morning to book an appointment. My take on it now is: If your body is screaming that there is something physically wrong, don't ignore it. As they say in yoga, "Listen to your body." My attitude at the time was that I was healthy and it was nothing serious, just clear fluid dripping out of a nostril, maybe caused by an allergy. I was very wrong.

It's miraculous that the bacterial meningitis didn't happen sooner. I had had this leak for at least four years, and had been travelling extensively for my curling and reporting careers. I travelled to Europe for curling numerous times, and covered the 2008 Summer Olympics in Beijing, China, for the CBC and then the 2010 Winter Olympics in Vancouver for NBC. I'm lucky the disease flared up when and where it did. It was fate that it happened so close to home and that I live near a hospital.

After telling the internal medicine specialist about the clear liquid that leaked from my nose, which I believed was brain fluid, he had an instant "aha" moment. He knew I must have had a small hole somewhere in my dura, the protective lining that surrounds the brain. I was sent quickly to an ear, nose, and throat specialist. He asked if I could produce a sample. I knew I'd leak whenever I did a downward-facing dog pose in yoga, so I did one there in the hospital room in my johnny gown while he held a sample cup under my nose. It took about five seconds for the brain fluid to start trickling into the cup. They got their sample and confirmed that I was losing cerebral spinal fluid. Now they just had to find the hole that was allowing it to leak. The first of several CT scans followed. They used dye so they could see everything better and clearly detected a microscopic hole in my dura. The small hole was just above the bridge of my nose, and that became the portal for the bacteria to get into my brain and cause bacterial meningitis. After years of joking about it, it turns out I actually did have an extra hole in my head.

Monty Mosher from *The Chronicle Herald* in Halifax called me five days later, while I was recovering in the hospital. He wanted to interview me about being inducted into the Canada Games Hall of Honour, which was happening in two months. I was being inducted with speed skater Catriona Le May Doan and sports builders Guy Rousseau and Jim Morell. Monty also wanted a few quotes about our upcoming curling zone playdowns, the first competition toward qualifying for the Nationals. I was due to be skipping a new team, and I explained to Monty that I wouldn't be able to compete in the playdowns because I was "under the weather with bacterial meningitis." We hung up the phone and then he called back a few minutes later to ask if, in fact, I had just said I had bacterial meningitis. He had clearly looked it up after he had spoken to me moments earlier. Suddenly he had a front-page story that was picked up by news agencies across the country (CBC, my employer, knew of my health condition, but was keeping it private).

A lot of people recognized me from TV, as well as from my curling career, and the story became bigger than I would have ever imagined. I started getting cards, notes, and flowers from curlers and viewers everywhere. My sister Monica works for the federal government and had people from different provinces asking about me and how I was doing. It was very touching. We were dealing with a big health scare, and I just wanted to focus on getting better. It was nice to hear from so many people who were worrying and praying for me, though.

The day after I was admitted to the hospital, we got hold of Luke in Florida and I downplayed things. We made sure he knew that I was just sick, and that even though I was in the hospital, my life wasn't in danger and there wouldn't be any long-term problems. After a couple of days in the hospital, Luke was able to call and speak with me. The meds had kicked in by then and I was feeling (and sounding) much better. When Luke arrived home from the sunny south a week later and saw me attached to an IV pole and wearing a hospital gown, he thought I looked horrible. But who doesn't look horrible in a hospital gown?

Even though I'd had something wrong with me for years, I hadn't addressed it properly. As I mentioned, a part of it was just my upbringing. My siblings and I grew up learning not to complain about things, and I felt reasonably fine. I also didn't want to be a burden on the health care system over what I thought was just a pesky runny nose. Before falling ill, I had been working on a story about the dangers of self-diagnosis. I talked to my producer, Jennifer Harwood, about making it a first-person story for the CBC, and she liked the idea if I felt I was up to it. So, from my hospital bed, I interviewed my internal medicine specialist, Dr. Rosario Rebello, for the piece. The story was broadcast across the country on *The National*. It was called "Being Dr. Google." I told a first-hand story of the dangers and folly of ignoring your body's warning signs and trying to self-diagnose through Googling.

AFTER I WAS released from the hospital, I felt like I had just woken up—first from the fog of my illness, and then from the sleepwalking of daily life. I promised to live a life of gratitude and calm. Mind you, there are still days when that's a challenge. But this "awakening" feeling has never left me.

Once I started feeling better in the hospital, I had so much energy and a feeling of such immense gratitude—I was just thankful to be alive. The nurse told me the feeling was probably produced by the steroids that had supercharged my body. But I felt so happy!

I can now look back and recognize that it was a crucial moment for me. A flashing sign telling me to enjoy life, to savour it, and to stop being absorbed in the small stuff that seems like big problems. I also began to realize that even though we like to think we have control of our lives, all we really have control of is trying to live an authentic life.

It's not that I was living inauthentically before my illness, but I was taking things for granted. It's funny, because I would go to yoga or meditation classes where the common theme is always to practise awareness, to be in the here and now, not in the past and not in the future. But I wasn't accomplishing that. I was being mindful for the hour I was engaged in the practice of yoga or meditation, but not totally embracing it in the other twenty-three hours of each day.

The moment of awakening I experienced has stayed with me and allowed me to detach so much more from the rat race—not just in a career sense, but also when it comes to regular day-to-day tasks. It is one thing to know that life is very precious, but another to learn that it is not worth worrying about the minor things anymore. Without the disease, and my recovery, I don't know if I ever would have truly woken up to this knowledge.

That's why the day I became sick was like a rebirth. In that moment, on that one day of my life, I had this amazing epiphany that life is precious and it can be over in a second.

And I realized the importance of taking advantage of simple things in life, like walking the dog or enjoying a cup of coffee. I was always doing several things at once: walking the dog while talking on the phone and having my coffee. I think this is something we all do. I thought I was being very efficient. I wore my type A personality and super-achiever nature like a badge of honour. Now I try not to take things for granted the way I think I was doing before. It's not that I wasn't enjoying my life, but I think too much of it was going by without me even noticing. Taking the time to just sit and enjoy my coffee seems like such a small thing, but in that moment I feel present and appreciative in a way I wouldn't if I was also doing (or trying to do) several other things at the same time.

My wake-up call was special to me, but I don't think these kinds of moments are unique. I think a lot of people have a similar experience when they are stricken by something that affects their health or the health of someone they love. Whether it's a heart attack, cancer, or a car crash, a lot of people realize in the blink of an eye the fragility of life. But once you experience this awareness, it changes your thinking.

I've always been a busy person. I have been competing in curling since I was a teenager, and I've never really slowed down. Being a part of the rat race doesn't necessarily mean always trying to climb the corporate ladder; it can simply mean that we're all busy staying one-up on everything. Once we get on the treadmill of life, it is hard to get off. We're all just sort of slaves to keeping the mortgage payments going, keeping the car payments going, making sure the kids are doing okay, buying groceries, doing the laundry, and so on. There are so many things we do every day to keep all the balls in the air, and the juggling is constant. My waking-up moment wasn't a realization that I had been doing things wrong, or working too hard—it was the epiphany that there is a delicate work–life balance and I didn't have to be super-woman 24/7. Of course, I still need to think about all of those daily things, but I don't need to fret about them.

Now I have balance—or at least I strive for balance. I try to tread a little lighter. My feeling is: Do the things that make us happy now, because tomorrow isn't guaranteed. Appreciate life, don't sweat the small stuff, and enjoy the ride. People say that all the time, but I plan to really live my life that way.

You can be a champion of the world one moment and gone the next. I can't help but think of two women who had been on my same curling journey, Canadian champions Marj Mitchell and Sandra Schmirler. Both died of cancer in their thirties. They were in the prime of their lives and curling careers. They had taught me a lot about curling, but their premature deaths taught me perspective. Even so, it took going through my own health problem to really make some changes in my life. When you're caught up in day-to-day living, it's easy to slip into automatic pilot.

My mother's two favourite sayings, which must be tattooed somewhere inside my brain, are: "Don't put off 'til tomorrow what you can do today" and "Here today, gone tomorrow." I now want to live by those words. If there's a trip you want to take, do it now. If there's a person you need to forgive, don't wait. If there's a dream you have, don't put it off. Live now. Curling taught me about competition and nurtured in me a desire to win, but my brush with a disease that had the potential to kill helped me to keep perspective. It might be my greatest victory of all.

CHAPTER 2
GROWING UP IN HALIFAX

I love travelling. I get very excited by seeing new things and tasting new foods. I am always imagining what places I might visit next, what adventures I want to have. I've been just about everywhere in the world, and I owe a lot of that to my work as a reporter with the CBC.

To cover the Olympic and Commonwealth Games, I've travelled to Russia, Australia, China, Korea, Greece, Italy, and my favourite, New Zealand. Plus, curling hasn't only taken me to every Prairie hot spot. I got to visit so many new places while throwing rocks: Switzerland, Sweden, Norway— all of which are stunningly gorgeous. As a family, we've hiked the Rocky Mountains and the Mayan ruins and all through Italy. But as much as I love new experiences, I'm always excited to get back to Halifax, Nova Scotia. It's where I was born, raised, and married, and started a family, and I can't imagine living anywhere else.

Nova Scotia is a really neat place. It's big enough to get lost in, but small enough to run into someone you know wherever you go. The landscape is ruggedly beautiful. You can go for a walk by the ocean any time you want and it quickly brings you to a state of Zen. We live pretty close to the water, and I see the ocean, smell it, and splash my toes in it every chance I can. On our licence plates, Nova Scotia is described as "Canada's Ocean Playground," and that is just perfect. Halifax is a city steeped in history; if you walk around in the downtown core, the old buildings, churches, and forts remind you of its early beginnings. The Halifax Explosion in 1917 is considered the worst tragedy in Canadian history. A French cargo ship, the SS *Mont-Blanc*, fully loaded with wartime explosives, collided with a Norwegian vessel, the SS *Imo*, in the Narrows, triggering an explosion that devastated Halifax. Almost two thousand people were killed by debris, fires, and collapsed buildings, and it is estimated that nearly nine thousand others were injured. To this day, we remember that tragic accident every year on December 6.

Halifax is very old for a Canadian city, and city planners protect its heritage. At the centre of the city is Citadel Hill and Town Clock, landmarks that draw tourists snapping photos and remind us of our military past and early beginnings. I love some of the quirky one-way streets, and the massive hills. And when the university students come back to town in September, the whole city is infused with a new energy.

Halifax is known as a friendly place, and it's hard to go anywhere without bumping into somebody you know. I think that probably doesn't happen as much in a big city. People here are more willing to talk to each other, and I like to think there's a little more humanity in a city when it's this size.

A cannon is fired off every day at noon from Citadel Hill. Where else in the world do they fire a cannon at noon anymore? No matter how long I've lived here, when that cannon blows at noon I jump a mile. And why do they fire it? It was the way they used to tell people back in the 1800s that it was lunchtime, and the tradition has lived on.

The who's who of Nova Scotia is pretty incredible: actors such as Ellen Page and the Trailer Park Boys; musicians like Anne Murray, Sarah McLachlan, Denny Doherty of The Mamas & the Papas, Rita MacNeil, Ashley MacIsaac, Natalie MacMaster, Hank Snow, and George Canyon; author Hugh MacLennan; and hockey star Sidney Crosby, to name a few. Alexander Graham Bell built his summer home in Nova Scotia and author Farley Mowat wound up living here. Once people start walking on Nova Scotia earth and smelling sea air, I think it is easy to feel that it's an authentic place where creativity can be nurtured.

And, just as important, the food here is amazing. We're right on the sea, so of course Nova Scotia is known for its seafood, particularly lobster, scallops, and clams. But it is also known for the Donair: meat inside a pita bun smothered with onions and tomatoes, with a special sauce, all wrapped up and served in tin foil. Honestly, it is the ultimate food for foodies.

Every time I've curled in a national event, I've been proud to wear the colours and crest of Nova Scotia. Some fans from Nova Scotia go to the national curling events and wear Sou'Wester hats and rain gear and even paint the tips of their noses blue. That's because Nova Scotians are called Bluenosers. The term was even added to the *Oxford English Dictionary* in 2013. There are several theories about the origin of the nickname. A popular explanation is that the term *Bluenosers* came from the famous Bluenose schooner, which was built and launched in Lunenberg in 1921. Another theory is that fishermen used to wear navy blue hats and mittens and the dye from the wool would get on their noses during the cold weather. Whatever the reason, we are Bluenosers.

Of course, as great as Nova Scotia is—and I know I'm biased—almost everyone here has a gripe about the weather. Certainly, it's not a perfect climate. In his book *You Might Be from Nova Scotia If...* cartoonist Michael de Adder depicts the four seasons in Nova Scotia: winter, spring, fall, and winter. But living here, you understand that. I was a weather reporter for fifteen years for the CBC, so I understand it all too well. But you know the old saying: "If you don't like the weather, don't worry: it will change in ten minutes." Well, that seems especially true here.

SO, I'M A BLUENOSER and a Haligonian (the slightly confusing term for people from Halifax) and proud of it. The Jones family has been here for a long time, too. According to family lore, my great-great-grandfather Jonathan Jones was in the King's Army, fighting in the War of Independence. He was injured in September 1776. In 1785, he joined the list of Loyalist families who wanted to leave the United States. They gave him a parcel of land in a place called Baddeck, Nova Scotia, on Cape Breton Island. There is a plaque there in town saying he was the first settler of Baddeck. That's how that side of the family wound up here. As for my mother's side, they were all named MacDonald, or so the family legend goes—I don't think there was a non-MacDonald in her family tree—and they took the boat over from Scotland way back when and settled in the Antigonish area. They all stayed there until my mom moved to Halifax. So, when I say I'm from Nova Scotia, I mean it.

Where we grew up in the west end of Halifax, it seemed everybody knew the Jones girls. When I went to school, I was never called Colleen; I was simply one of the Jones girls. At church, I was one of the Jones girls. Even at the grocery store, they knew me as a Jones girl. That's what happens when you are one of eight sisters born in succession, almost all with the same height and look, walking around in a part of the city where you could get to everything without having to drive.

We evolved as individuals in a large family, nurtured but never coddled. We were taught to work hard, pick ourselves up when we fell down, and keep moving forward. In a big family there is no time to feel sorry for yourself, and whining was not tolerated. All of these early childhood lessons served me well in life, but particularly on the ice in my curling career.

It might seem odd by today's standards to have eight girls in a row and then finally my brother, Stephen, for nine kids overall, although we knew families in the neighbourhood that had ten or eleven kids. In our neighbourhood, we had many families with five, six, or seven kids. But we were definitely the only family to have eight girls and one boy. In today's world, if someone told you they had nine kids, you'd maybe bite your lip in sympathy. But back then it wasn't that unusual. I must admit I was a little envious of smaller-sized families from time to time, especially their trips to Disney World—that magical place I have yet to visit—but not often.

In that run of nine Jones kids, I was number five. I was born on December 16, 1959, and named after a sister who had passed away shortly after birth. She was actually the twin of my older sister Maureen, but was just too small to survive. Naming me Colleen was my mother's way of remembering the baby who didn't live long. My birthday also fell on the anniversary of my paternal grandfather's death on December 16, 1932. Are other people's births so connected to others' deaths? I remember more than once coming downstairs as a youngster, saying, "It's my birthday!" and my dad would say, "And the day my father died." Not said in a negative spirit, but just as a factual sentence.

My dad, Malachi, was a lawyer who became a judge. My mother, Anne, ran the house. And as I've said, what a house! Roseanne came first, then came Barb, Maureen, Sheila, me, Monica, Jennifer, Stephanie, and last but not least, Stephen. The first five girls were each born a year apart, after which my parents took a "break." Beginning in 1961, the final four children were born within seven years. My mother gave birth to Stephen at age thirty-nine. It was only when I became a mother myself that I realized how hard it would be to parent nine kids. My husband, Scott, and I had all we could handle with two, Zach and Luke, born seven years apart.

My parents were no strangers to large families. My mother had five sisters and brothers, and my father had seven siblings and was raised by a single mother after his dad passed away from a massive heart attack when my dad was just two. As kids, we never asked my parents why they had so many children—were they determined to keep trying for a boy, or maybe it was because of their Catholic faith? Kids today might ask their parents those types of questions, but it wasn't on our radar. We were born, we were thankful, and we had a massive household. I can't imagine raising nine children, but it was a different era, and I often joke that there's no way that I, as number five in the pecking order, would be born today.

So, what was it like growing up in a big family with nine children, two adults, two dogs, and a cat? In a word: chaotic. We had a lot of female energy in our home, and mostly it was fun. We always had lots of company, and we were all friends as well as sisters. But, we all had different personalities. Barb and I joked around a lot together, and were often referred to as "the funny ones." I hope my sisters meant that as a compliment.

We lived in a big house with lots of bedrooms, lots of noise, and nowhere near enough bathrooms. I roomed with Monica because she was the next youngest. Monica would tell you that anyone who knows both of us would say we are opposites, but we had so much fun together and we'd laugh really hard. Monica recently told me a story she remembers: One time, when we were kids, Mom and Dad drove us down to the Yarmouth ferry. Before they put their eleven- and twelve-year-old daughters on the ferry by themselves to Maine (we were being met on the other end by our Aunt Lorette, who lived there), we spent the night with our eldest sister, Roseanne, in Digby, where she was working for the summer at the beautiful lodge there. We went out for dinner and Roseanne let us eat all of the desserts on the menu. Afterwards, Monica and I went swimming in the pool and we were laughing so hard that we almost drowned, just from being silly or on a sugar high—not sure which one. There were no lifeguards and no parents, just the two of us trying to save each other.

Even so, Monica was really the more responsible one, and Dad would tell her to look out for me and keep me in line. That wasn't really fair for a younger sister, I suppose. Monica jokes that she left home for university at eighteen just to get her own room. Maybe this is only a half-joke. Monica was always more organized than me. I was the chaotic, more messy one, but I learned soon enough that when the mess got really bad Monica would clean up after me.

We traded more than chores, though. I tended to buy more clothes and collect more things, but we shared everything. I guess the difference is that when she borrowed my clothes, she'd put them back in some order, whereas I would just leave her stuff on the floor. I like to think I'm much more organized now. I've had to be, with my own family and career. But as a kid, it was just my nature to be messy.

Bathroom time was shared between all the girls. I didn't even think it was normal for people to be in a bathroom by themselves. You couldn't possibly get that many children out to school in the morning without having four people in the bathroom at the same time.

The house was busy all the time with friends always coming and going; it was never a quiet family life. Growing up in a family of nine children is as close to commune living as it gets. Clothes were shared, passed down, and patched. You learned to put away your things (I tried, at least), play nice, and share. Those three traits have stayed with me.

Meals were eaten around a giant kitchen table that sat all eleven of us. When supper was done and the dishes were finished, a net was placed in the middle of the kitchen table and table tennis games followed. There were chores to be done, but there was never an assigned list. We just pitched in to get the laundry folded, the dishes washed in assembly line fashion, the floors swept, and so on. I realize now that I was pretty much born in the Mesozoic Era compared to my sons. We grew up with a two-channel television set and a dial-up phone, and in a time when parents would throw you out the front door in the morning and tell you they'd see you at supper. How lucky we were! All that free time to imagine, create, be bored, explore, and get dirty. The idea of video games back then was like something out of a science fiction book.

Parents who have smaller families probably wonder how my parents did it. As a parent myself, and with the benefit of hindsight, I realize that every day my parents were just trying to get by and survive. I can't imagine what it would be like to have nine kids. Having met other people from big families, I've realized that the parents are the head of the organization but it's the siblings who raise and fend for each other. God bless Roseanne; she was like a second mother in our family. But we all instinctively looked out for one another and raised each other.

When I was two and a half years old, I went down the street to call on a friend, Kenny Almond. No one was home, so I turned to go back down the stairs, took a tumble, and cracked my head open. Blood was spilling everywhere, and my then five-year-old sister Barb, who was outside playing, heard me crying, picked me up, and took me back home. My mother, unfazed and seeing no limbs missing, applied pressure to the gaping hole for hours. I probably should have gone to the hospital, but Mom was too busy looking after a pile of kids and managing the house to do that. As adults, there are things we look back on in our childhoods and wonder, *What the hell?* But at the time we didn't think much about it. I guess it was perfectly normal that my mother didn't take me to the hospital. She was a pretty unflappable person, and it would have taken a broken bone poking out of the skin for my mother to have decided to go to the hospital. To this day, no hair will grow on my head where I had that one-inch gash. What I learned from this early crash was to watch my step and pick myself up quickly, while applying pressure.

In a big family, you become very resourceful and independent. If you don't grab your piece of the pie, you're never going to get it because there will be nothing left. While most of my sisters and I ran cross country at school, we weren't brought up in a competitive sports environment. Yet because of the size of our family we were always competing in one way or another. We would compare ourselves in terms of school marks, clothes, cross country running—anything. And it wasn't just us. At school, if one of the Jones girls made the honours list, the teachers held all of us to that standard. That was only natural, I think, with so many of us so close in age. Competing was a foreign concept to my parents, so we didn't grow up with that killer instinct. In a big family like ours, we just learned to figure out the systems—and to keep our Gordie Howe elbows up.

Sometimes in a big family mistakes happen, including missing out on a Christmas present. I can appreciate that being Santa for nine kids is a huge job, but twice my Mom miscalculated. The first time was when I was twelve. While everyone else found their pile of presents, there wasn't one for me. I promptly brought it to Mrs. Claus's attention, and she told me to look in the den. I was thinking to myself, "Yes! It's probably a new bike." But nothing was there. I came back into the living room and Mom had arranged a crokinole board game and the whistling Roger Whittaker album. She said to me, "There is your pile, you just didn't see it." I do remember my disappointment, but I kept a stiff upper lip even though I believed I'd been forgotten. I knew better than to voice it. My mother would have said something like "Be thankful you have a roof over your head and food on the table." I'm sure, as a Depression-era kid, she had some pretty lean Christmases in the 1930s and 1940s. She wouldn't have thought that missing out on the latest toy was a big deal, but darn it, I did want the Easy-Bake Oven! It was harder to bite my tongue when it happened again the next year, but I did. Like many from their generation, my parents had sayings about the value of money and being resourceful. Their favourites included "waste not, want not," "a penny saved is a penny earned," and "save money for a rainy day." They also referenced the "stiff upper lip" quite a bit. My father's favourite saying was "stop friggin' and jiggin' 'round." In other words, go get the job done and stop complaining.

I sort of buried those Christmas debacles until my own children came along. Then I took the role of Santa very seriously. There were lists to be made, checked, and double-checked. Scott would beg me to stop buying presents, and I would say, "Well, I want to have enough. There should be a decent pile." I know the meaning of Christmas is not commercial materialism, but a few presents to celebrate the season are the custom. To this day, I have kept the Roger Whittaker album I received when I was twelve. But as my mother would say, I should really "accept, bless, and move on."

Our childhood had an innocence about it. We were united, and there weren't any fights because fighting wasn't tolerated. My parents wouldn't put up with us not getting along or not being kind to each other—not even with angry words. They would use Catholic guilt to make us all love one another. I would say that my parents had a strong faith. They were very religious. We had a painting of Jesus in the hallway and crosses placed strategically around the house. We always said a prayer before eating—all of us at the same time.

My father, who passed away in 2013 at age eighty-three, was sturdily built, standing six feet, and had a very strong personality. As a father to eight girls, he quietly pushed feminism on us long before it was in vogue. Little wonder, since his father died when he was two and he was raised by a single mom. We hadn't heard of women's liberation, but he was all about books, career choices, and learning to take care of ourselves. If we were competitive at anything it would have been school, as Dad was always clear on how important it was for us. He always wore a tailored suit, never owned a pair of jeans or sweatpants. He even wore a pair of dress pants when he relaxed at home, and old dress pants and an old dress shirt when painting the interior or exterior of the house. He loved to walk—a good four miles each way to work. He'd leave after we all had breakfast and he'd be home by 5:30 or 6 p.m.

He taught all of us to ride a bike, and I recall going on bike rides with him on Saturday mornings. He bought a Norco ten-speed bike for himself in the early 1970s, when cycling wasn't big, and single-speed CCM bikes for us to share. I don't know why he did it but I'm glad, as that's what led to us biking on Saturdays and gave me a lifelong love of cycling. The two of us would stop for an ice cream at the old Farmer's Dairy as part of our trips. This was the only one-on-one time we could get, and I treasured it. When I was cycling with him, I learned to find peace on two wheels. No talking, just riding. I don't remember everything we did as kids, but those bike rides are crystal clear. I'll always remember my very first bike—one I didn't have to share. It was a three-speed beauty with a cool banana seat, monkey handlebars, and hand brakes. Then there was my first ten-speed—a Mercier with suicide gear shift, located low on the frame—which I bought myself with babysitting money. It was stolen shortly after I bought it, and I was devastated. I never did get it back, but I saved my money again and upgraded to a Peugeot. I started going on longer rides. This is when I discovered that if I was stressed or needed time to think, cycling allowed me to restore my mind and hit the reset button.

Dad loved other sports and activities, too. We owned a modest twenty-three-foot sailboat—my father christened it the *Jennifer J*, after my sister Jennifer—and were members of the Armdale Yacht Club and the Waegwoltic Club. I would often go sailing with my father because he needed another crew member. Maureen regularly accompanied us, as well. I don't sail anymore, but when I'm on the water kayaking I find it incredibly peaceful. Dad found a lot of relaxation out on the water. He was a worrier, which he came by honestly. His mother was also a worrier and she came from a long line of worriers. Being so young when his father died, my dad's introduction to the world was probably something like "bad things happen." He grew up in the 1940s in Rockingham beside the Bedford Basin, which was home to the Canadian Navy and supply ships. The fear of attack during World War II meant that everyone's lights had to be out at night. So great was the fear that Halifax port might be attacked, his job as a young teen during the war was to ride his bike at nightfall and yell, "Lights out, lights out!" through his neighbourhood. No wonder he became a worrier.

He graduated from Saint Mary's University and then Dalhousie University's law school. He had a lengthy career in government as a senior solicitor, and was appointed to the Supreme Court of Nova Scotia in 1970 and to the Court of Appeal in 1979. He retired from the bench in 1998. He lectured at Saint Mary's, taught criminal law and procedure at Dalhousie for many years, and was awarded an Honorary Doctor of Laws from Saint Mary's University in November 2003. His father and also his brother Dave were lawyers. Of all of us, only Barb followed him in that path. My son Zach is now pursuing law, continuing that family tradition.

Dad taught us that everything could be solved with a healthy walk, a bowl of hot porridge, a good book, a long bike ride, or time spent in the garden. He loved to read and to garden. He started an incredible rose garden in the back-yard and then a vegetable garden, too. Now, I look back with some amazement at the things he did. Carving out quiet time is something each of us learned to do—it was important to find a little corner of private space somewhere in the house or outside where there was no noise. The fact that he was ever able to do that with all of us children running around is remarkable.

My mother is a beautiful lady with crystal-clear blue eyes and the kindest heart. She wore her hair like Queen Elizabeth. As much as my father did, she did no less. Mom was a really busy woman, managing a full house. She made bread, pies, everything. Nothing came out of a package in her kitchen. She sewed our clothes and school uniforms. She was a kind, generous woman—the type of person who welcomed people into her home with apple pie and tea—and everybody loved her. She was a very nurturing, wonderful mother. When I became a mother, she was always offering to babysit and bring over food. If there was any trouble—say, someone was cranky—Mom would get us all together, have us kneel, and make us pray. Maybe that sounds odd, but I look on that now mostly as a meditation for her. Before we went to sleep, growing up, we all said our prayers.

From my mother I learned an important rule: "Blessed be the peacemakers." She would recite this any time it seemed that life in our family zoo was getting out of control. And she meant it. She wanted us to make peace. I imagine that, being the mother of nine, she dreamt of peace and quiet. I could really fill a book with the little poems and sayings my parents would recite. I used to think they were all their own little quotes. It was only later I found out that "Love all, trust a few, do wrong to none" was not an Anne Jones saying, but rather William Shakespeare.

We lived about half a kilometre from school and always walked. We went to a Catholic school and wore finely pressed uniforms. My mother had an assembly line of sorts, to make sure all of our uniforms were pristine and clean. If you had a hole in your sock, it wasn't thrown out; it was darned. She taught us how to do that. With eleven people in our house, every day was wash day, and she didn't use a dryer. She hung everything on the line. It probably took her forever just to get through the breakfast dishes. She was always busy.

Every day, we had the same breakfast—hot porridge, toast, orange juice, and coffee—and it was prepared by my father. There was no Cap'n Crunch. We had no idea those types of cereals existed. We'd see things like that during sleepovers at friends' houses and they were alien to us. We didn't know cereal came in a box. We just figured that porridge was the only option for breakfast, and that was what everybody ate. My parents did what worked and what needed to be done to get through each day. I will say that while I grew to hate porridge in my teen years, it is now a daily part of my diet.

So, Dad made breakfast and Mom made lunch and supper. It was non-stop for her because we'd all come home at lunchtime, my father included. Lunch was the big meal of the day. My parents believed in that expression of eating breakfast like a king, lunch like a prince, and supper like a pauper. (Another regular quote from them that actually can be attributed to Adelle Davis, not Anne Jones.)

Every summer, my parents took two weeks off and we'd rent a cottage near some beach. We always went to Bayfield or Mahoneys Beach, which was part of the Antigonish community where my mother grew up, or to Stanhope in Prince Edward Island. At that time, parents did not ship their kids off to summer camps. There were no camps, so it wasn't even an option. We never got away from each other, and I laugh now thinking about that. Some of our friends growing up spent vacations in Disney World and came home with all sorts of stories about this magical-sounding place that was very different from Mahoneys Beach. It sounded better, but we had no way of knowing if that was true.

We'd all pile into the back of a wood-panelled station wagon that did not include seat belts or air conditioning. We'd count heads to make sure no one was left behind. But one time we did forget Stephen, the baby of the family and much adored by his sisters, who all considered themselves to be his mother. We turned around after two minutes when roll call revealed he wasn't there. The cottages we rented were a mere step above sleeping in a tent. There were two bunk beds in each room and it was cramped. The cottages at Mahoneys Beach had no running water and an outhouse that we were terrified to use. But we always had fun getting sunburned on the beach, playing our favourite summertime sport "kick the can," and jumping waves. Before today's world of being connected 24/7, there was a time of made-up possibilities, sandcastles, boredom, and dreaming.

Because there was so little room in the station wagon, my parents allowed us each to take only a small knapsack of clothes, which included a pair of shorts, a T-shirt, some pairs of underwear, and a bathing suit. The only other thing we packed was a dress, because we always went to see the epic production of *Anne of Green Gables* at the Charlottetown Festival. It is the nation's longest-running musical. I've seen *Anne of Green Gables* eleven times and it always made me cry. I was also inspired each time. It was a big highlight of our summers. Although it might seem boring to kids now, we loved it. I grew up idolizing Anne Shirley for her pluckiness and perseverance. She was my childhood heroine. I still see the musical every time I'm on the Island and love the character that Lucy Maud Montgomery created. Anne might have been fictional, but what a great role model she was. Never giving up was imprinted on my soul, thanks to her.

Both of my parents seemed to believe that the devil finds work for idle hands, so we were taught to always be busy and doing something. I think we inherited that from them. What we didn't inherit from them was a desire to throw forty-two-pound stones of granite down a sheet of ice toward the rings called a house at the other end. The Joneses were about to discover something new and become a curling family.

CHAPTER 3
THE GAME

Curling wasn't a part of our family repertoire, but it quickly caught on. For my parents, it got a lot of kids out of the house in a hurry, and at about twenty-five dollars per kid for the winter it was a really inexpensive sport. Now, most kids begin curling because that's what their parents do, but that wasn't true in my case.

We began curling at the Mayflower Curling Club, which became the club where I curled for most of my career. The Mayflower, founded in 1905, has a storied history that goes way beyond throwing rocks. In 1912, it served as a morgue for victims of the *Titanic*. When the recovery boat brought the deceased to Halifax, they put the poor souls in the ice shed because it fulfilled two needs: it was big enough and cold enough. I'm pretty sure we are the only curling club in the world that has ever been called on to meet such a request. Back then, the club was on Agricola Street, about a ten-minute walk from its current location. Sometimes, when a shot goes wonky, I think the spirits of those lost on the *Titanic* must have moved with the club.

I HAD NEVER heard of curling until my sister Barb was invited by a neighbour, Karen Fitzner, to go to the Mayflower Curling Club. Karen and her family curled a lot, and Barb was hooked immediately. One by one, as we each turned the magical age of fourteen and were eligible to join the junior program, we followed Barb to the club. First it was Maureen, then Sheila, and then finally, in 1973, it was my turn. Monica, Jennifer, and Stephanie all followed when they turned fourteen. Only my oldest sister, Roseanne, and the baby of the family, Stephen, didn't play. They preferred that other ice sport, hockey.

The reason we couldn't join the curling club until age fourteen probably had something to do with the fact that to play, a curler has to throw a forty-two-pound hunk of granite down the ice. Today, there are junior stones that weigh half as much as the regulation forty-two-pounders, so kids start curling at age five and six now. Not to sound too much like an old-timer, but they have really enhanced teaching tools for young players who are learning the technical and fundamental side of the sport. Curling is a lot like golf in many ways; there are so many strategic nuances and it's a hugely mental game. So, one by one, we made our way to the curling club. But it wasn't just a matter of turning fourteen; we had to wait for an older sister to give us the nod. It became a rite of passage, and something the whole family could celebrate, in a sense. My mother discovered this was a fantastic thing because the first game started at seven on Saturday morning and we were gone until one in the afternoon. Even though they didn't understand the game, my parents soon realized what a godsend this curling was. We were out of the house all day.

My parents didn't curl and rarely came to the club. In hindsight, this allowed us to flourish without the behind-the-glass coaching I witnessed from other parents. My parents tried to understand the game, but they were so shocked that any of us turned out to be so good at something that they were just in awe. Also, they were raising nine children, so they were as far from being umbrella parents as it gets. It wasn't that they didn't care; they just considered curling our play time and didn't interfere. They cared about us doing our homework and getting our chores done, but not about this Saturday thing called curling.

We always walked to the club, which was probably a solid half-hour walk and brutally cold in the winter. The kids born in the second half of our family eventually started getting drives as the older ones left the house to go to university—fewer people around meant that we could enjoy some luxuries, like Mom and Dad giving us a drive in the old wood-panelled station wagon.

Curling is all about precision shot-making, skill, and for sure some luck, and I have experienced all of these in my career. Curling is played on ice by two teams, each with four players: lead, second, third or vice-skip (or mate, as we call it in Nova Scotia), and skip. Each player throws twice, alternating throws with the opponents. Curlers throw rocks down to the opposite end of the ice, aiming for the rock to slide and stop in the rings called the house. The house is divided into a twelve-foot circle, an eight-foot circle, a four-foot circle, and the smallest circle in the centre, called the button. The object of the game is to get your rock closer to the button than your opponent. Once all sixteen stones have been thrown, the "end" is complete and a score is recorded for that end. The teams then turn around and throw the rocks back to the house at the other end of the ice. In national and world competitions, the games go to ten ends, and if a game is tied it goes into extra ends. I've always compared an end to a baseball inning, except in curling either team can score.

Curling is a grand old game invented by the Scots in 1541. It's a little like shuffleboard, a little like bocce, and a little like pool with all the angles. There is a lot of skill involved, and a lot of strategy. It is appropriate that the game is called curling, because that's what the rock does—it curls. To make the rock curl down the ice, a slight twisting motion is added before letting go of the handle on the rock. By applying either an in-turn or an out-turn, the thrower can make the rock curl one way or the other as it moves down the ice. While the rock is travelling, teammates sweep the ice in front of it to help control the curl plus drag the rock further. The yelling that goes on in a curling game are directions to the sweepers, usually to sweep faster and harder. But the strategy is the key to it all, which is why curling is often called chess on ice. You can throw a "draw" if you want the rock to end up in the house, or you can throw a "hit" to remove your opponent's rocks from play. Like golf (also invented by the Scots), there are many shots in between the hit and the draw. There are a ton of strategy decisions to be made in the course of a ten-end game, all of which will affect the outcome. This is the quick beginner's guide, or Curling 101.

When I was a kid, the Mayflower Curling Club had six sheets of ice and it was always freezing inside. The ice was crazy-heavy and slow. There were a couple of reasons for that. They did not have what's known as jet ice back then, and icemakers were still learning all of the tricks to making good ice. And no one in the 1970s understood the importance of the rocks. We were probably playing with slow, dull rocks that were unmatched (not consistent). Not that we knew any better. It took all my strength to heave a rock down to the other end of the ice. We swept with old corn straw brooms, which were like a skinnier version of a kitchen broom. The one I used was called the Little Beaver—that was actually what the manufacturer named it. It made a wonderful slapping sound on the ice, something missing with today's push brooms, which have a synthetic head designed to make it easier and more efficient to sweep the stones.

The Mayflower had a junior program for kids every Saturday morning. The ice was fully booked through the week with league curling, so Saturday mornings were junior time. There wasn't a lot of training going on, just kids figuring it out and having fun. I was not a natural at the game by any means, but I did love it right away. There was something about being all bundled up in a big wool sweater, being out with your friends, the hum of the ice machine, and getting to yell, "Hurry hard!" to urge your teammates to sweep harder. Like the old-style brooms we used, we didn't have top-notch equipment.

Curlers use special shoes, for instance. One shoe has a Teflon slider that allows you to push out easily and slide in a nice, smooth delivery, and the other shoe has a gripper on it that allows you to push off from the hack. But back in the 1970s when I began, I didn't have a nice slider. Instead, I used electrical tape on the bottom of my left sneaker as a slider. Electrical tape was pretty primitive even then, yet it probably allowed me to develop a relatively solid slide because it slowed me down much more than the modern

Teflon used today. My slide was slow but technically strong, and I came out nice and square. The kids who start on Teflon fly out of the hack (the starting point where you push off) with little control and sometimes a bit sideways.

I was slow to figure out certain things about the game, like strategy. Even the difference between an in-turn throw and an out-turn throw confused me. The turns determine which way the rock curls down the ice and are a huge part of the game. The out-turn always came more naturally to me, and it was clear early on that I could use it well. It's probably the only turn I threw for the first five years I played. Throughout my career, my bread-and-butter shot has been the out-turn hit.

I didn't have a clue how to curl at first—not even an idea—because I never saw it on television. I learned the rules and the basics at the club, but I never saw the strategies and different skills used in competitive games. In the games we played on Saturday, our strategy consisted of you trying to land one in the circles and your opponent trying to take it out. It still makes me laugh sometimes that I became a curling broadcaster and live in an era in which curling draws huge TV numbers and can be watched on the internet. Growing up, we simply had no access to any of this. There were no televised games except the Brier final and an 11:30 p.m. show during the Brier called *Brier Night Live* that I wasn't allowed to stay up to watch. There was no one to learn from but the people around you. My sisters showed me how to slide on the kitchen floor before I actually started going to the club. Our kitchen had that old linoleum floor and, using the cookie cupboard as a hack, we would do our best to mimic a slide wearing just our socks. We didn't get too far with our pretend slide, but it sure did help our form.

Before too long, we very much became a curling family. When we weren't on the ice we were practising sliding on the kitchen floor or flapping our corn brooms down in the basement. Together, we talked a lot of curling strategy around that kitchen, table tennis, and homework table. At first, our strategy was not very sophisticated. It was pretty much to hit everything in sight as hard as possible. This was the 1970s and 1980s, well before the rule changes in the early 1990s that allowed for more rocks to be in play. Prior to the rule changes it was hit, hit, and hit some more, so there were fewer stones in play. But with the introduction of, first, the three-rock rule and, later, the four-rock rule, the strategy totally changed. The four-rock rule is simply that the first four rocks in an end that land in the free guard zone cannot be removed from play. The free guard zone is the area between the hog line and the rings. With more rocks in play, there is much more strategy. I remember watching a 2–1 finals in the Brier in the 1980s—2–1! No wonder they introduced rule changes. Curling had become like watching the NHL's neutral zone trap made famous by the New Jersey Devils: not exactly exciting.

Growing up in the family cocoon, my curling skills were nurtured within the safety net of my sisters. A healthy competition developed between us where we wanted to be as good as or better than each other. Before long, our junior program expanded to after-school practice and soon I spent a ridiculous and wonderful amount of time at the club throwing a lot of granite with my sisters and friends. I didn't understand the game at first, and I didn't know how to get better. I sought whatever help I could. I read *Ken Watson on Curling*. Watson was a three-time Brier champion who is known for developing the long slide. I loved the old black-and-white pictures of Watson throwing with what looked like an old kitchen broom, a fedora on his head, perfect dress pants, and a solid-looking slide. His was a simple book with simple ideas, but I memorized it from cover to cover. His seven *C*s of curling are still ingrained in my mind: confidence, compatibility, co-operation, competitiveness, courage, consistency, and concentration. I still talk about these qualities when I coach juniors. They are what Watson believed was needed to be a champion, so I worked hard to find, keep, and hold on to all seven. While there have been many changes to curling—from the gear, to the ice, to the rule changes—since Ken Watson's time, his seven *C*s remain true.

CURLING SOON BECAME more than a game to me; it became an obsession. I was growing more competitive and became restless to improve. It all came to a head in 1976, when I played in my first Canadian Juniors tournament at seventeen years old. Let me tell you, it was a big leap going from playing Saturday morning curling with friends and family to a Canadian championship. I played second on a team skipped by Kathy Myketyn, who was based across the bridge in Dartmouth, along with my sisters Maureen and Sheila. People ask me today how the team was formed, and the truth is that I don't know exactly. My sisters and I figure that the juniors coordinator, the late Mac MacKinnon, got a call saying that Kathy was looking for three curlers, and it was our good luck to be standing in front of him at the time. All I know is, we eagerly said yes. Not that I really understood what I was getting involved in. I was pretty green about it all.

We may have had only a couple of practices together. Kathy came over to the Mayflower Curling Club for those. Suddenly, we were playing in "the zones," the tournament that begins the qualifying process leading up to the Nationals. We somehow won the zones. As with every game I played in my juniors, I was sick to my stomach with nerves beforehand. This was a pattern for me, one I probably didn't overcome until I was in my forties. Anyhow, we won the zones and advanced to the Provincials in Springhill (famous as the birthplace of Canadian songbird Anne Murray). I didn't even know what a provincial championship was. I was still having trouble telling the difference between an in-turn and an out-turn. There was a blizzard-like snowstorm that day and we were trailing 7–4 with three ends to go. Mostly everyone had gone home, thinking our opponents were going to win, but we rallied to win 8–7. It was like a Cinderella story. We were excited to win the Provincials, of course, but I was also excited just to win a curling iron in a junior Christmas bonspiel. (Really, the first prize I won in 1975 was a curling iron for my hair. I've also won toasters, pots and pans, sweaters, drills, coolers, beer steins—you get the idea.) My level of excitement would have been the same even if this hadn't been a provincial championship. I was happy to win, no matter the prize. When we were told we were going to the Nationals after winning the Provincials, I had no idea what to expect. I hadn't realized that winning this competition would mean going on to a bigger one. This first major competition is a blur. We don't even have a picture to commemorate the moment. I was simply along for the ride, doing what my big sisters told me to do.

The Canadian Junior Curling Championships is a week-long event that takes place in a different city each year. That year, it took place in Thunder Bay, Ontario. I clearly remember getting out the *Encyclopedia Britannica* to figure out exactly where that was. Three weeks after winning the Provincials, our parents piled us into the station wagon and drove us to the airport. They weren't curlers, so they couldn't tell us what to expect. When you come from a curling family—like my husband, Scott, did—you know the progression of the tournaments. But back then, we were just Saturday morning curlers at the Mayflower. We were rookies at all of this.

This was also our first time ever travelling on an airplane, so we were doubly excited. We were going on a grand adventure to this thing called the Canadian Junior Curling Championships that took place in the Port Arthur Curling Club in Thunder Bay. You never forget your first airplane trip, and while we weren't nervous, we were pretty wide-eyed during takeoff. Sheila, Maureen, and I sat side by side and tried our best not to scream with excitement over this whole flying thing.

When we got to Thunder Bay, we marvelled at the snowbanks and the cold. Sure, Halifax gets lots of cold and snow, but Thunder Bay gets more. We settled in and got ready to start curling. But we *weren't* ready. For starters, we weren't used to playing two games a day. Plus, because we were sweeping with corn brooms, my hands bled hard after awhile. What I remember most about that first day, though, was that we were losing and that was torture. I had always loved winning, but I think my absolute hatred of losing started there in Thunder Bay at those first Canadian Juniors. We lost the first two games 14–6 and 9–6, which even by today's standards are ridiculously high scores. I felt better when we won the next three games in a row, but then we lost our last four. I remember looking at the other teams, and thinking that they seemed really professional compared to us. We played like we had just fallen off the turnip truck.

Maybe it wasn't just that the other teams were more professional. We stayed in an old hotel and even though three of us were sisters, we all felt extremely homesick. Maureen says the experience brought us closer as sisters, and I would agree with that. But this was our first time away from home, and we missed it. We called our parents on the hotel's phone, sitting in a closet, telling them we wanted to come home. I can still remember telling them: "We need to come home. We hate this. This is horrible." I don't know if it was the losing or being on our own for the first time that led us to feel that way. I think they told us to buck up, and so we did.

We had gone from the Mayflower Curling Club with our buddies to the Nationals, and it was just too big a leap. Today, things would be different. We would have been coached all season and we would have had meetings with a sports psychologist. We would have been ready. Today's junior curlers have their eyes wide open, partly because of the level of coaching and partly because the competitions are televised, so competitors have a chance to see what the event looks like beforehand. But we were young, naive, and clueless.

I was only seventeen years old and thinking about it now, I'm amazed. As trying as the experience was, I somehow became completely hooked on curling. Curling is a lot like golf in that it is very addictive and seems to call to some people. Well, curling was screaming at me. My sister Barb and I had curled together a lot, and she became instrumental in my career. She even took a course in coaching and passed her knowledge on to us. When we came home from Thunder Bay, Barb took me to the club to work on the things I needed to improve. She fed my curiosity for the game and continued to do that each time I returned from a national tournament, win or lose.

Something else happened to me after the experience in Thunder Bay. I knew going forward that I had to skip. If I had to endure the torture of these games, I wanted the pressure of throwing that last rock. I knew I needed to get a whole lot better, but I was chomping at the bit to be as good as the teams I had seen in Thunder Bay. Somehow, a skip was born through our losing experience there. After being exposed to curlers from across Canada, I had a better understanding of how to improve my play. So, something was ignited at those Nationals and it sparked a desire in me to get better. A lot better.

The following year, after Thunder Bay, I formed my own team. My sister Sheila was with me and I picked up Colleen Chisholm and Shelley Blanchard, who was from Dartmouth but living in Halifax at the time. I initially called Shelley thinking that she was a nice person and a good curler and that she'd be a great teammate. Colleen proved to be a good fit because she was very smart and very quiet. It's always good to have a quiet one on the team who will go with the flow. We went through the same process as the year before—zones, then Provincials—but this time I felt like a seasoned veteran. I practised all the time—not so many team practices, but I threw a lot of rocks. We won the Provincials and were heading back to the Nationals. This time they were in Saint John, New Brunswick. Barb made the trip with us, acting as our coach, and this helped a lot. She organized our schedule and scouted the other teams. These were things we had seen the other junior teams do the year before at Nationals and it helped. We finished with a 6–4 record. Even so, Cathy King and her Alberta rink (or team) were dominant, winning the championship. In later years, I would play against Cathy many times at the national women's competition, called the Scotties Tournament of Hearts, and then again at the Canadian Senior Curling Championships. So far, she's the only female curler to win the Nationals at all three levels: junior, women, and senior. That is such an awesome record to hold.

Those Nationals in Saint John were my first as skip and my first playing with a team I had formed myself. I'd had high expectations and while we did well, we didn't win. In some ways we were still too amateur a team. We were missing some of the competitive drive that I was so hungry for. But I was slowly figuring out how the system works. We needed four great players who practised all the time. At that time, Nova Scotia did not have a strong curling program. We figured out by being at the Nationals that we needed to throw a lot of rocks and work really hard.

It was only after losing at the Nationals a second time that I became very hard-core about finding the best players. I put together a team for the 1979 Canada Winter Games that included Sally Saunders (my future sister-in-law), Margie Knickle, and my sister Monica. Of all of us Jones sisters, Monica and I stuck with curling the longest. We were both pretty intense about the sport. Monica is also a born optimist, so she fights until the end of every game. That was what I needed on my team.

Sally and Margie were both from Lunenberg and were really solid players. We had a coach now in Joyce Myers, and she really guided us. Joyce was such a terrific mentor who spent countless hours developing players. She organized practices and most of all was so positive in everything she said to you. She was truly inspirational to so many female curlers in Nova Scotia, and she certainly spent a lot of years guiding me.

We went through the playdowns in Nova Scotia and eventually won to move on to the Canada Winter Games, which were in Brandon, Manitoba, that year. As with Thunder Bay, we had never seen so much snow or felt such bone-chilling cold. The Canada Winter Games are a really cool experience for a young athlete. For starters, we were housed together with athletes from all of the other sports in dorms at Brandon University. The Canada Games are like a mini Olympic Games for Canadian athletes, a first experience playing in a multi-sport event.

Unlike my first time in a national tournament, we were now working as hard as the so-called top teams. Our practices looked professional and we walked like champions. We were on a roll in Brandon and finished first in our division with a 5–0 record, advancing to the final against Denise Lavigne's New Brunswick team. Denise had skipped her squad to three consecutive Junior Provincial titles, and I knew it was going to be a hard game. We had seen them play in tournaments in Nova Scotia and they were really well coached for that era, considering that the idea of coaching was still relatively new in our sport. The game was tied 3–3 after five ends, but I had a bad miss in the seventh end that really cost us the game. As Monica recalls it, Denise's team was "really in the zone." We lost the game 7–4, and I remember being absolutely steamed about losing the gold medal. It's only in hindsight that I can look back and see that losing gold was the best thing that could have happened. It motivated me in a big way to push a little harder, to get better, to throw more rocks, and to learn from these tough losses. There was definitely a silver lining to that silver medal.

I thought we had done everything possible to prepare. Maybe we had, but remember that this was 1979, well before curling blossomed into what it is today with its massive television coverage, video technology to watch your games, technical-training programs, improved equipment, and coaches who specialize in mental training. In 1979, curling was very much still in its infancy in terms of player development. All of that has changed, but back then the onus was on you to get better by sitting down and just going through the game in your mind, shot by shot, trying to figure out what went wrong. We would draw house circles on paper and sketch out scenarios. At restaurants, we would use salt and pepper shakers and ketchup bottles to describe a scenario we had in our heads. It was pretty primitive stuff.

Throughout my career I never handled losing well, but in my younger days it went beyond that. Basically, it led to a huge depression and a lot of soul searching. I measured my self-worth according to wins and losses. I wouldn't be able to sleep because I would replay entire games in my head, shot by shot. As a skip, I have always felt the losses were entirely my fault, either by missing a shot or by making bad decisions in strategy. In hindsight, I learned a lot from the defeats. But did I really need to mentally beat myself up that badly? Maybe it made me stronger; I'm not sure. Through the years, I've worked with a lot of sports psychologists to learn how to be a little easier on myself. It was Ken Bagnell who ultimately found the way to turn all of my negative internal bashing into positive thoughts. He was our mental coach from 2001 to 2006, during which we won four national women's titles in a row and our two world titles. I am so grateful to him for everything he did for us. My guess is that any athlete will tell you that dealing with losses is an emotionally draining exercise. It has been a lifelong process for me. I don't think anyone is born knowing how to handle it all. It's better just to win all the time, but that's pretty much impossible.

Immediately following the Canada Winter Games, I flew home from Brandon and started preparing for the Canadian Women's Curling Championship—then called the Macdonald Lassie—because I had signed on to play second for Penny LaRocque. (The Macdonald Lassie would become the Scott Tournament of Hearts in 1982 after a sponsorship change.) Penny was a veteran skip who recruited me at nineteen years old to play on her team, and I was eager to learn the ropes from her. Penny had won the Nova Scotia provincial women's title the year before and had been practising at the Mayflower. She noticed I was out on the ice as often as she was. I think that impressed her, so she kept an eye on how I developed as an athlete. I'm guessing she knew it wouldn't be long before I was skipping my own team, so she invited me to play on hers. So, I was playing on two teams—skipping my own, which headed to the Canada Winter Games, and playing a different role for Penny. It was kind of "a bird in the hand is worth two in the bush" sort of thing. The Lassie was held a week after the Canada Games. I was going to Dalhousie University at the time, and tried to squeeze in a few classes in a semester that wasn't getting much of my attention. I knew the team I was skipping was strong, and I also knew I could learn a lot from Penny and would benefit from playing second stone.

Penny was a wonderful mentor for me because she was way ahead of her time. She was very positive, believed in training, and was timing the rocks. Timing the speed of the ice with stopwatches is commonplace today, but was unheard of back then. The stopwatches gave you a real idea of the speed, rather than the old way of just saying "it's keen" or "it's heavy." Penny also believed in practice, practice,

practice. We would throw practice rocks—draws and hits—and simulate game scenarios. This was something I had been doing with my junior teams, but she took it to a new level for me. Penny used other methods, too. One time, she invited a yoga instructor to her home to teach all of us how to relax. Penny believed that was really important for dealing with the anxiety of competition. It was all trial and error, because none of us knew what we were doing. While I love practising yoga today, I had never even heard of it then. In 1979, there certainly wasn't a yoga studio on every corner like there is today. The instructor began and at one point we were all lying on the floor in the living room. It was meant to be relaxing, and we were supposed to be taking it very seriously, but I just couldn't help myself. I started giggling, just like when I was a kid at home with my sisters. I lost control. The giggles became snorts, which means I had fully lost control of myself. I felt bad for Penny; I wanted to impress her, but the more stern and serious she became about the whole thing, the more I laughed. Still, despite the giggle incident, I truly did learn a lot from Penny about what more I needed to do to improve my game and my state of mind. Using visualization in 1979 was way ahead of what other curlers were doing.

Penny's team also included Brenda Shutt at third and my sister Barb throwing lead stones. Barb replaced Charmaine Murray, who had to withdraw from the tournament because she developed mononucleosis. Charmaine's bad luck would be my good fortune. Because of our age difference, Barb and I had never played juniors together, so it was wonderful for us to be on the same team at last.

There wasn't much time between the finals at the Canada Winter Games and the start of the Lassie, which meant I couldn't dwell on what had happened or even rest up. I made a quick stop in Halifax before heading to Montreal for the Nationals. It was cool to suddenly be with my sister at the Nationals, because she was the one who'd got our family interested in the sport. She also motivated me to get better. Curling with Barb was really neat, because in our family we supported each other totally, and Barb had a way of making me laugh on the ice. I'm a different person when I'm curling. I'm normally a very light and free person, but I was always deadly serious on the ice and everything was do-or-die. Barb provided me with much-needed comic relief at the perfect times.

Surreal is probably the best word I can use to describe that first experience playing in the Canadian women's championship. I think a big part of that was because it took place in Montreal, which isn't a city that traditionally has a huge curling following. Curling is certainly nothing like hockey there. Though the sport has grown in Quebec, it still hasn't reached the levels in the central and western provinces. And, at that time, Canadian women's curling was a small-time event compared to men's curling. The women's Nationals was still in its infancy, and this particular event took place in an old arena—until then, I had only played in clubs. There weren't many people in the stands. The tournament didn't really become a big-time event until Scott Paper Limited came on board as the title sponsor in 1982 and put a lot of resources into it. So I didn't feel nervous that first time. Not only did I feel I belonged there but I also felt I was better than the other players. I knew that this was where I was supposed to be and that I was really good. I felt the confidence that so many young athletes have, even though it was my first year in the tournament. That competition had eleven teams representing the provinces and territories, and the favourite to win was British Columbia's Lindsay Sparkes, who had won the Nationals in 1976. It was pretty neat to be in the same field as Lindsay. She had been my idol after she won in 1976, so to have the chance to play against her was amazing.

I can't remember all the specifics of that tournament, but I do remember that we finished with a 7–3 record, tied with four other teams for second place. As a result, we ended up in a complicated tiebreaker to qualify for the playoffs. We wound up losing 8–5 to Manitoba. In the end, Lindsay Sparkes and her team won the whole thing.

I learned a lot from Penny in that year and admired her work ethic. After the tournament, I wanted to return to skipping my own team again. That was where I felt most comfortable. I learned one more thing from playing with Penny, though. When I left her the following year to form my own team, I knew I was going to have to outwork her. We remained friends, but we always knew that we'd have to beat each other from that day on. Penny, of course, won the Canadian women's championship in 1983, and I think the healthy competition between our teams helped both of us develop.

THAT WHOLE curling season, and especially the period between December and March with the Canada Games and the Lassie, was a whirlwind because of the amount of curling I did. Yes, it was a dream season getting to play in my first Canadian women's championship and the Canada Winter Games. I have no complaints about that, but it definitely affected my schooling. I was in my first year of a Bachelor of Arts program at Dalhousie University and went straight from the Lassie to school for exams. I'd learned nothing, because I hadn't been to any classes. I couldn't possibly study and do all that travelling. Mind you, Barb managed to get a law degree during all of her training and competing. Clearly, she was better at time management and was studying between games. I never was the organized one.

I became so obsessed with curling that I didn't have time to focus on my schooling. I thought I could go to classes and curl competitively, but it was impossible. There was a curling event every weekend, not just the Provincials and the Nationals. My parents never said anything to me about not concentrating on my education, because I don't think they knew how obsessed I had become with the game. They would see me heading out to the Dal library, but didn't know I was reading the *Winnipeg Free Press* and *Edmonton Journal* to study every tournament going on in Manitoba or Alberta. I don't know how many eighteen- or nineteen-year-olds were doing that. You couldn't buy those papers in Halifax, but Dalhousie University had every newspaper in Canada—some stacked on little poles, others on top of one another—and there was only one copy of each. I would read articles on Winnipeg's Kerry Burtnyk, who won the 1981 Canadian men's championship in Halifax at nineteen years old, and Edmonton's Paul Gowsell, who won the 1976 and 1978 World Junior Curling Championships and later skipped in the 1980 Canadian men's championship. They were young, rising stars who I thought I could learn from, but I also wanted to get some information about this game that I loved. There is no other word for it than obsessed. In Halifax, curling was a Wednesday night hobby; it certainly wasn't a big thing. It's big here now, but wasn't then.

We had a good Canadian championship with Penny, but I remember looking at Barb during the competition and saying, "I need to skip." It wasn't anything to do with Penny;

I just loved skipping. Barb agreed, and that boost of confidence from her led to us forming a team the next year with me as skip, Sally Saunders playing third, Margie Knickle playing second, and Barb as the lead. This was basically the Canada Games team, with Barb replacing Monica because Monica was still junior age and not eligible for the women's yet. We clicked instantly and again, after going through the zones, we moved on to the Provincials and won. We were on our way to the Nationals again, this time in Edmonton.

Unlike Montreal, curling is huge in Edmonton, so the Nationals immediately felt different. Even though I was skipping, I felt the same confidence I had the year before in Montreal—like I really belonged. Among the squads in the tournament was New Brunswick's, skipped by Denise Lavigne, who had beaten me in the finals of the Canada Winter Games the year before, and Ontario's Marilyn Bodogh, playing third for her sister Christine—they would go on to win the Canadian and World titles in 1986. I remember how I felt there in Edmonton in 1980. I was confident, and felt ready. It had been only four years since my first Canadian Juniors in Thunder Bay, but I had worked so hard at my game since then.

The round robin portion of the championship was exciting and intense. Barb recalls that this was when we first experienced what could be described as a hostile crowd. In her words, it was "quite frightening," because it was as if everyone in Edmonton showed up for our game against the Alberta team. We definitely felt like the underdog and lost that game. But we recovered from that and finished first overall with a 9–1 record, and advanced to the finals.

There, we experienced playing in a nationally televised game for the first time. CBC had made a commitment the year before to televise the Lassie, but only if the tournament changed to have a three-team playoff format. Previously, the winner of the round robin was crowned the champion, and there was no finals or championship game. Television was moving into the sport and wanted a different playoff format to create more interest. This caused a huge debate in the curling world, a sport steeped in tradition. Should competition change to something as wild as playoffs? We take it for granted now, but it was a significant change then. But the course was clear: The Canadian Curling Association knew that in order for the game to progress it needed to embrace playoffs. That year in Edmonton, the first year with this new playoff format, four teams tied for second place with a 6–4 record and so we had a couple days off before the finals while they played the tiebreaker round. We waited and watched to see who our opponent would be.

We didn't just watch, though. We knew that the squad that won the tiebreaker was going to be a tough team, and we needed to prepare. The late Hec Gervais, a two-time Canadian champion and world champion from Edmonton, took us to his club to practise. He was known in the curling world as the Friendly Giant because of his massive physique. Hec, who had more or less adopted our team, thought the long break for us, while the other teams fought it out in the tiebreakers, would wreak havoc with our game. Bless his heart, he took us under his wing. At that time, the Canadian Curling Association didn't have any practice ice at the arena, so we were very grateful to Hec for taking us to his club. No practice ice at the arena where the championship is being played is a crazy concept today, but remember that these were the early days of the sport. The idea of playoffs in curling was still brand new. The sport's growth was only just beginning. The practice time at Hec's club did keep us focused over those two days. But what we didn't realize was that the club had totally different ice than the tournament arena in terms of speed and rocks. We would soon discover the impact this would have.

I slept little before the finals. This would become a pattern before all big games: lots of nerves, little sleep. We were all really nervous to be playing in our first Canadian finals before a national television audience. We were in awe of the television lights and the tracking camera, set on the carpeted walking area between the sheets of ice, that followed our delivery. It was as if Hollywood had moved in. When TSN came on board in 1986 to televise the entire round robin, it gave players a chance to get used to the lights-and-cameras experience. But in 1980, this was brand new for all of us curlers.

So, playing in the finals for the first time was totally different. Now it was one game with built-in television drama. Ernie Afaganis was the host for CBC, dressed in that salmon-coloured jacket that CBC announcers wore back then. He stood at ice level and talked in a booming voice, throwing it to the broadcast booth where Don Wittman and Don Duguid were calling the game. Sometimes Afaganis would lead into a commercial break, even if you were getting ready to throw the final shot of the end. You just had to try to block him out. Meeting him again years later, when we were both covering a Canada Summer Games in Kamloops, British Columbia, I told him, "You know, Ernie, that was just a little distracting for me!"

It was pretty freaky, and I think it's safe to say we were all scared to death. As Barb recalls it, all the hoopla going on around us had us feeling pretty tight. The playing of bagpipes that is part of the introductions for the final game, the prize trophy on display, and the prospect of a trip to Scotland for the world competition if we won were overwhelming when added to the lights and cameras. And the competition was tough. We played Saskatchewan's Marj Mitchell, who scored two in the first and stole one in the third. They were a much more experienced team than we were. We did rally and I even had a hit for three, but I really botched it and ended up giving her one. I still don't know how that happened. We were down 5–1 after five ends, but rebounded in the second half of the game, trailing 6–5 in the tenth end and needing to steal a point to force an extra end. Stealing in curling is when you score even though the other team has the advantage of last rock. We came so close, but it didn't happen and we lost. To this day, that game is a bit of a blur and one that seemed to move in such fast motion, as if it took all of five minutes to play. All I really remember is Ernie Afaganis throwing to commercial breaks in his salmon jacket.

When the game was done, we stood on the podium and were given medals. Standing on the second-place podium is no fun. I know we're supposed to act like there's nothing wrong with winning silver, but I will never buy that. In curling it is very true that to the victor go the spoils. If you win, you get a lot—beginning with going to the Worlds as Team Canada—and if you lose, you don't get anything other than a "thanks for coming out." Only the team that wins is remembered.

Marj and her team went on to win the Worlds in Perth, Scotland, and although I wanted to be there to compete, I was happy for her. Sadly, she died three years later because of cancer. She was only thirty-five years old. Now, the Marj Mitchell Sportsmanship Award is given out annually at the

Canadian women's championship. I really didn't know Marj, except for playing against her in that final, but her death shocked me.

After our loss in the Canadian finals that year, I was devastated. I've said I always took losses hard, but this time I really went back to the drawing board, trying to get better. Joyce Myers, who represented Nova Scotia in many national competitions and was later inducted into the Canadian Curling Hall of Fame as a builder, was terrific for us. She was a Canadian Curling Association–certified coach and had complete and utter confidence in me. She was really passionate about the game and believed in me totally. I was lucky to have her working with me. Curling coaches volunteer so much of their time, and Joyce spent many hours with us. But when I think back to those days, the coaching tools were still pretty primitive. We couldn't watch games on videotape and start dissecting what the opposition had done because the technology wasn't around then. We just hashed things out face to face around a table, drawing diagrams. At least we had evolved from using salt and pepper shakers to illustrate scenarios, but not by much compared to current methods! Today, by using video analysis of games and deliveries, players can improve faster. Plus, there's so much to learn from the detailed statistics gathered at every game—it gives players a better understanding of how to improve.

Joyce was a huge help, but in the next year, 1981, we didn't make it back to the Lassie. We bowed out really early in the playdowns, losing in zones, the qualifier for the Provincials. I don't remember what happened, but we must have all played really, really badly. To not get out of our city was shocking. I don't remember if the ice has been bad or what, but considering the success of 1980, we imagined we'd walk through the Provincials. Maybe that was the problem. Either way, we didn't make it through and that was devastating. As crushed as I was, this wasn't the first time I'd lost something. By now I was realizing that there was a lot to learn from losing. Mostly it was to work harder and practise more. Think of the number of golf balls Tiger Woods must have hit on the practice range to reach the level he did. The same is true in curling. You need to throw a lot of rocks and set up a lot of practice scenarios in order to get better.

And that's exactly what I did.

CHAPTER 4
A FRESH START

After losing in the zones in 1981, I knew we had to come back strong. It wasn't so much that I doubted myself, but rather that I wanted to build on our 1980 success. The 1982 season would become the launching point for my career as a Canadian champion, but at the time I was focused only on my next game. Even though we hadn't qualified and moved past our city playdowns in 1981, we kept the same team together. I had a hunch there was something good about it. The vice-skip, Kay Smith, who skipped Nova Scotia to a Canadian junior championship in 1980, and my sisters Monica and Barb were keen and hungry to win. We had great chemistry and Kay fit in well with the trio of sisters.

Mind you, the Provincials didn't start out so great. We lost our opening game, and because of the double knockout draw our backs were up against the wall right off the bat. A double knockout draw was standard in the 1980s. All teams start on the "A" side of the draw and when you lose one game, your team falls into the "B" side. When you lose a second time, you are out of the tournament. So there was a lot of pressure on us quickly when we lost early on the "A" side. A feeling of déjà vu crept in. But after that opening loss, we found our stride and won the Provincials to earn a trip back to the Nationals, this time in Regina, Saskatchewan. We were poised to win the title that had slipped from my grasp two years before. I was a pretty confident, maybe even cocky, twenty-two-year-old who believed that if I was runner-up in 1980, the next logical step was to win the thing.

Scott Paper Limited had just come on board as the tournament sponsor, and this revolutionized the event. To start, it became known as the Scott Tournament of Hearts, later the Scotties. Robin Wilson, the second on Lindsay Sparkes's 1976 and 1979 Canadian women's championship teams, had been a former employee of Scott Paper—in fact, the company's first female salesperson—and had been approached by Bob Stewart, Scott's group vice-president of marketing, to put together a proposal for sponsoring the event. The company wanted to broaden its scope into some form of event marketing in addition to its specific brand advertising. Curling was extremely popular in a lot of smaller communities across the country, and Bob saw that women in sports were growing and still an untapped market in Canada. He contacted John Leonard, head of the company's advertising agency, who called Robin. The men's national curling championship, the Brier, was already extremely popular, and Bob wanted to raise the profile of the women's tournament to rival that. It really was quite visionary, and so began the era of women's curling that helped it become what it is today. Bob also wanted to create a brand legacy that would stand the test of time. The story goes that Robin and her sister, Dawn, devised the name for the event while drinking a bottle of wine at their mother's house. The new logo for the tournament featured a circle of four hearts, because a heart is worn on the uniforms of provincial representatives in the Nationals. The four hearts also symbolize the four players on a curling team and the camaraderie that exists between them.

The rebranding of the tournament intended to include the name Scott in all media, promotion, and advertising. It took awhile to gain traction—Robin says the tournament's new name met with initial unrest because it sounded like a parade or a poker tournament—but it did catch on and soon became as well known as the Brier, with television numbers that rivalled the men's event. Right from the beginning, Bob had a vision that women's curling would become the premier women's sport in Canada. And it has. That was a very special year for the sport in Canada, and for me as a competitor. I suppose we all had something to prove in 1982.

It was an amazing change, and only those who played in the 1970s or early 1980s can fully understand the metamorphosis that happened when Scott Paper came on board. Canadian women's curling was about to change in a major way because of this sponsorship deal, and the curlers who played in the tournament reaped the benefits of it. Robin became the tournament coordinator, and being a former curler, she knew what needed to be done to take care of our needs while also helping to raise the profile of the women's game. We were all made to feel important. The tournament went from a low-profile, minor event to a major one, and I marvelled at the change. We had fashionable team outfits, catering, and drivers to take us from the hotel to the arena and back again—all provided by Scott Paper. Each player who won her province or territory received a gold necklace with a pendant made up of the four-hearts logo. Then, after each additional Provincials you win, a diamond is put within one of the hearts. Eventually they had to come up with new prizes, because we won more than four Provincials and our pendants filled up. So they made an amazing tennis bracelet that looks like the pendant. Every day, someone mentions my gorgeous jewellery to me. What a wonderful idea the necklace was to kick things off.

There were a lot of first-class changes to the game and Robin Wilson and Scott Paper had the vision to see how much women's curling could grow. The most important change was having the foresight to put the tournament in nice arenas instead of minor hockey rinks. They also spent the first year promoting and marketing the event, and the fans started coming out and filling the arenas. It was the women's game that started the Team Canada concept; it's a terrific marketing strategy for the event and it helps build heroes in the women's game. That first 1982 Scott Tournament of Hearts championship was held in the Regina Agridome, in a city that captures the very heartbeat of curling.

The new uniforms we received had our names on the back, which made us feel like the pro athletes we were. With no first initials to differentiate the Jones sisters, there were a lot of Joneses out there. But for me, it was more important to wear the Nova Scotia crest. The first time I went to the Canadian women's in 1979, I remember looking at the crest with amazement. If selfies had been around back then, I would have taken a few of them. It felt great to represent Nova Scotia, and that feeling never changed no matter how many times I played in a national tournament. It's a special feeling, representing your home, and it never gets old.

Having Barb and Monica on the team in 1982 allowed me to be very open. We've always been very supportive of and honest with each other. I could say anything to them, and they would always understand and forgive me. This was the advantage of playing with my sisters. We knew what we could say to each other and get away with; it was a release for me as the skip. And considering that I was still a young twentysomething with no mute button, it was nice that if I was overly critical about our performance, they knew to let me get it out. Barb became a good sounding board and was my go-to person when I needed to vent. She always knew how to bring me back to a neutral or calm state. If she saw I was becoming mad or too tightly wound because of missed shots, she knew how to lighten the mood with her goofy Monty Python impersonations, or just bring me back to normal in some other way. And that was great. Kay fit in really well with the three Jones sisters; she was a pure thrower and added so much to the team. Monica always saw the positive in any end or any shot; not only was she a solid shot maker, but she was also the cheerleader or rah-rah person on the ice. I think we all knew, as with any team, that we were dependent on each other and that each of us brought something different to the team. They knew, though, that because I was the last rock-thrower, they had to keep me relaxed and in a happy place. Their attitude was: We're a team and we should keep our skip happy because she plays better that way.

I attracted attention at the tournament by wearing a Sony Walkman during practice. Nobody else was doing this. This was the latest gadget in the still mostly technology-free 1980s. One article written at the time described me as a "rock music fan from Halifax." I had started using the Walkman in 1981 at the Mayflower Club to get into curling mode, listening to Bruce Springsteen music that I had recorded on cassette tape. It was my way of psyching myself up—remember, this was long before the era of sports psychologists and coaching tools that have become part of the mental preparation and focus of athletes. Now it's not uncommon for athletes in all sports to listen to music with earbuds or headphones before the start of a game. But at that time, wearing headphones while throwing practice rocks or during a game was pretty much sacrilegious. Curling was very rooted in tradition, and the sport was already changing so much.

Because we'd been in the 1980 finals, we had a different attitude and disposition in 1982. In a word, we were more prepared. We were ready for the cameras and the pressure. Mind you, this would be Monica and Kay's first time in front of the cameras, but at least Barb and I did our best to prepare them and give them ideas on how to ignore it. We tried to stay relaxed through the week, and one way we achieved this was by chewing gum. We had read that chewing gum helps concentration. Chewing gum was something I continued throughout my career, just to stay loose and help me concentrate. Some fans hated it and said we looked like cows; others mailed us what seemed to be a lifetime supply of gum. Barb was sick throughout the Nationals, battling strep throat and taking antibiotics, but as she says now, "The show had to go on." So there we were: me with my Walkman on and all of us chewing gum. We were able to stay loose, and at the end of the round robin we were one of five teams tied for first at 7–3. This was an unprecedented result in the twenty-two years of the tournament.

I was still smarting from our final round robin game, in which we lost 7–6 to Ontario in extra ends. We were playing Carol Thompson, and she made a great shot, drawing to the button and bettering two of our stones that were in the house. It was a tough loss, because if we had won that game we would have gone straight to the finals. I didn't talk to the media afterwards, which is considered a cardinal sin. As I matured, I learned the importance of talking to the media. Not only do they have a job to do, but with women's curling still in its infancy then, media coverage was only going to help the sport grow. My team and Dot Rose's from Winnipeg had the best records in head-to-head play among the teams that tied for first, but we were declared the top team because we had beaten hers in the round robin. I was so upset about losing to Ontario, but as it turned out, the game wound up not taking us out of first place after all.

We faced Saskatchewan's Arleen Day in the semifinals, and because she curled out of the Royal Caledonian Curling Club in Regina we had to contend with the hometown crowd. And what a crowd! It was full of fans wearing Saskatchewan green, with cowbells and signs. I was not prepared for this. In our finals in Edmonton two years earlier there had been maybe five hundred people watching, and that seemed like a lot. Now there were five thousand, and they all seemed to be cheering for their Saskatchewan team. Luckily, the Day rink was probably as overwhelmed as we were by the sight of the huge crowd. We started strong and never looked back, winning easily 11–4. That was a bit of a shocker; they were such a strong team and I wasn't expecting such a lopsided game. But I was relieved to get it. We faced Dot Rose's Manitoba team in the finals. Not surprisingly, Dot had won her semifinals game also. She'd played lead on Betty Duguid's team from Manitoba that won the tournament in 1967. She played in the tournament again in 1969 and a third time in 1973 (this time as the second), losing in the finals. So here she was, nine years later and fifteen years since winning the Nationals, looking to win her second title. Our team had an average age of twenty-two, the youngest of all the teams in the tournament. We were up against a lot of experience, plus there's always something intimidating about playing against Manitoba teams. It's like they were weaned on curling rocks from birth. They produce champions like no other province.

The game started well for us. We scored four in the opening end and I thought it was "game over, hand us the trophy, and let's start the party." But, oh no. They scored three in the second end and another one in the third end to tie it up.

That is when I started questioning myself. I was getting nervous and tighter. They led 6–5 at the fifth end break and two ends later the score was tied again. We were hanging on by our fingernails, and I had this sinking feeling that history was about to repeat itself. After coming all this way, was I going to lose in the national finals again, just like in 1980 against Marj Mitchell? It was gut-check time and we just gathered ourselves and started making shots. Nowadays, in this kind of situation, when feeling uncertain, I can draw on mental preparation and sports psychology. Today, players can even take a timeout and talk to their coach, but back then we were on our own to figure out how to stop the bleeding. We were sort of twisting in the wind in terms of how to be tough and stay mentally strong. Even the way the game flows now, with breaks between every end and the coach sitting at ice level and having the ability to talk to the skip or other members of the team—that wasn't part of curling in that era. All we could do was keep playing and try to work through our difficulties. This is a big problem that faces every athlete: learning how to handle the pressure and how to perform when it matters the most.

The tide turned for us in the eighth end. We stole a single point, forced them to take a single point in the ninth end, and had hammer coming home, meaning we had last-shot advantage in the final end. What does all of this mean in plain English? Curling has often been described as chess on ice. Often games are won or lost in the final three ends. As a skip in a tight game, you are trying to control the scoreboard. You desperately want last rock coming home, because then the game is in your hands. To get that last rock, you have to force the other team to score in the ninth end. For me, more energy and thought goes into controlling those last three ends than any other part of the game. It's like the final two minutes of a tight NBA game, when it's all about ball possession and the shot clock. The same is true in curling.

With the game tied and us in control of the final end, I was in the position that every skip wants: the chance to win it all with the final shot. To win, I needed to remove the opposing stone in the house and keep my own stone in the rings. It's called a hit and stick, the kind of shot I had practised millions of times at the Mayflower Curling Club. I needed to throw an in-turn hit, and as I've said, my best shot is an out-turn hit. My in-turn had a tendency to curl a little when I didn't want it to (that might be an understatement), and I remember telling myself to just throw it clean. I remember the feeling of sliding down the ice to the other end. My heart was racing. I paused before I went to throw and took a huge breath. I slid out. I knew I had made the shot right from my release. It was perfect. I leaped high in the air, arms over my head, and ran to hug Monica, Barb, and Kay. I'll never forget that moment. It was pure jubilation, exaltation, and gratification all wrapped up in an instant. It was truly one of those moments when time stood still.

At twenty-two, I became the youngest skip in tournament history to win. I remember the absolute joy of winning and realizing I had probably spent five years visualizing that very moment. It was definitely a huge turning point in my life to win that tournament.

We were paraded in front of the crowd, accompanied by bagpipers, and it was an incredible feeling. There are two moments that stand out for me, things I'll never forget. One was this moment: walking out in front of the crowd, down the centre sheet, as the champion. Everything inside me was vibrating with energy, right down to my toes. I can't compare it to anything else. And to be able to do that with my sisters? Amazing. When the bagpipers are playing, the arena is electric. Everyone is cheering the victory. And those bagpipes just send goosebumps to every part of my body. We were all in tears over what we had just accomplished.

The other moment I'll never forget is walking into an arena for a national championship for the first time. These arenas don't look like hockey rinks; they're places of magic transformed into curling rinks. From the flowers that line the arena to the carpet that surrounds the sheets, the transformation is always magical. It always feels like a place just for me.

When we won, it was front-page news in Halifax. People were unbelievably excited. Curling wasn't on anybody's radar in Halifax back then (except perhaps in the Jones household), although a year later Penny LaRocque won the Nationals and that was a big deal. Nova Scotia certainly wasn't like Manitoba or Saskatchewan, where it seemed everybody curled. When I got home, I had to explain to people what the tournament was, so that was kind of funny. There was a party at City Hall and a party at the curling club.

I HAD FINALLY won the Nationals, but we had no time to relax. We had just two weeks to get ready for the World Curling Championships in Geneva, Switzerland. We were pumped about making our first trip across the ocean and heading to the land of chocolate. There was so much to do. We didn't even have passports. It was a whirlwind of preparation and we were on such a high that it was hard to stay focused. The women's Worlds were still a relatively new event—the first one had been held only a few years earlier, in 1979—and we had no idea what to expect.

For the first time in my career, I would be wearing the uniform of Team Canada with the maple leaf on my back. I didn't think it possible, but it was even more special than wearing the uniform for Nova Scotia. I was always so proud to represent Nova Scotia, but now I was representing *everybody*. It dawned on me that, in a way, I had won for all curlers in my country, and that took the experience to a whole new level. We were no longer competing just for ourselves or our hometown, but for the entire country. We were swamped getting ready. From passports to outfits to practising, there was a lot to do in a short time. It was the farthest any of us had ever travelled, and after we arrived in Geneva, that five-hour time difference knocked us out for the first few days.

While we had a lot of anticipation for the Worlds, they proved to be a completely different experience. In terms of organization, it was an absolute nightmare compared to the Canadian championships. As I said, the women's Worlds was still a new event. This one took place in a massive arena but the crowds were small, and those who did attend all seemed to be ringing cowbells. That is pretty standard in Switzerland; it's their way of getting into the spirit of sports, but it was just a little distracting.

There were ice issues and each end of the sheet of ice had its own guessing game as to what weight to throw. It appeared to be sloped. It could be keen and fast going one way, so that the rocks would travel very quickly, and heavy going the other way, with the rocks grinding to a stop. We figured the surface wasn't flat, but had no proof of that since no one at that time used stopwatches to time the speed of the rocks. I just knew in my gut that there was something wrong with the ice. Plus, at one end of the arena were big windows through which the sun shone brightly into the building. This definitely seemed to have a big effect on the ice as well.

I felt like Alice in Wonderland falling down the rabbit hole, because we were helpless to do anything about it all. We knew we were struggling from the outset and had no confidence in the ice; we had no idea how to make shots. Still, we managed to win our first game 12–3, beating Ruth Schwenker of the United States, followed by victories over Italy, Scotland, Denmark, Germany, and France. Our winning streak ended with a 6–3 loss to Sweden's Elisabeth Högström, who had won the tournament the year before. Then a different sort of streak began. We followed up our defeat against Sweden with losses to Switzerland and Norway. Once the slide started, we had no idea how to right the ship. We were in well over our heads. While I think the ice conditions affected everyone, the European teams and the Americans were used to playing on sub-par ice conditions. Things have changed now, but back then Canada was light years ahead in pioneering ice-making techniques. So we were spoiled. When we got on bad ice, we really had no experience with how to handle it. For the Europeans, bad ice was second nature. It never even occurred to us to use a stopwatch to determine the speed of the rocks and whether there were any changes in the ice conditions. The next year, Penny LaRocque started using stopwatches regularly and I wish we'd had that foresight. But it wasn't on our radar.

In addition to the issues with the ice, we were still adjusting to the time change and were exhausted from all of the planned events and functions. This was not unusual for curling back then, when the organizing committee wanted to have opportunities to show off their city to the curlers. But it seemed we were always being whisked from the ice directly to a chocolate fondue event or a wine and cheese party. Meanwhile, all we wanted to do was sleep.

I became so frustrated that I just put on my Walkman and tuned the world out. It wasn't a good reaction. We were assigned a Team Leader, appointed by the Canadian Curling Association to act as a liaison between ourselves and the World Curling Federation. Dawn Knowles of British Columbia, who I had played against in 1979 when she was on Lindsay Sparkes's team, became our Team Leader, but we really didn't know her. Coaching was still a really new concept for a curling team. We met Dawn in Geneva, not having had any time with her leading up to the tournament. She certainly couldn't fix my downward spiral, so the Walkman became the only answer. But even Bruce Springsteen didn't help.

Our Worlds wasn't going very well for us, but I'd remembered the importance of speaking with the media. I did daily radio interviews over the phone with CJCH in Halifax. Maybe this was where I got a taste for broadcasting, but at the time it was just part of the whole experience. I'd always loved telling a story, and when Chuck Bridges, news and sports director at CJCH, asked if I would phone in reports from the World Championships, I thought, *Sure thing.* I would talk about my experiences that day, how we had played and what the competition had been like. Clips from those interviews were lifted and used for the news and sportscasts during the rest of the day. It was unique at the time, because mostly only sportscasters described what was going on. This was one of the few times there were actual reports coming back from someone who was in the thick of competition. It was very similar to how athletes use Twitter today, but back then it was novel. The radio station did a great job of bringing a different perspective to covering sports, and I was proud and happy to be a part of that.

I also wrote a column and dictated it daily to *The Chronicle Herald* in Halifax. I was reporting on myself, describing a lot of the same things I talked about in the radio pieces. In hindsight, perhaps it was not a good thing to be doing while trying to win the World Championships. I don't think this media work hindered my performance—you get used to doing a fair number of interviews as a curler. But I had jumped into the reporting with both feet because I was already thinking about trying to work in the media. Maybe I took on too much, but the reporting helped to focus me when I was feeling down.

In any event, although we were in a downhill slide, at the end of the round robin we wound up in a tiebreaker with Norway. We were still struggling with the sloped ice conditions that we never figured out, and lost 8–6. It seemed to happen so fast—and just like that, we were out. We'd failed to qualify for the playoffs. It was only the second time in the men's and women's World Championships that a Canadian team had been eliminated so early. It was a dismal result. Canada is always expected to win, because we're a curling nation. When that game ended and we hadn't done well, I felt like I had let down the entire country. I knew the expectations that went along with being the skip of Team

Canada, but I had no idea of the feelings I would have after the tournament ended. As a team we definitely felt down together, but I still think that for a skip the feeling is worse. The skip calls the shots and decides the strategy, so I always felt there was something more I could have done—one great shot I could have made to turn things around at a crucial moment that just never came.

LOSING AT the World Championships was like never even winning the Nationals. Somehow, the big win back home that I had been obsessing over for years and finally achieved felt hollow. The World Championships was still new for women, but Canada was expected to win nonetheless. That pressure still exists today, but it is a little different. Now, when Team Canada loses, the feeling is that the other countries have caught up to us. But in the early 1980s, it was more like Canada *had* to win.

We imagined the people following the tournament in Canada were probably in disbelief. This was before the era of Twitter, Facebook, and online comments, so we didn't have to worry about their reaction just yet. If Canadians were disappointed, we didn't know it. We were in our own little world and knew only how we felt. I'd gone to the Worlds feeling the combined strength of all Canadian curlers behind us, and we knew that we had let everyone down. Nobody could have been more disappointed than us. After the loss, we locked the dressing-room door and refused to allow the three intrepid Canadian journalists there to interview us. For all my involvement in media for the tournament, and aware-ness of their importance, I just couldn't face it. As a reporter now, I hate it when people don't give interviews when the going gets tough, but I can always understand it. We did eventually open the door, but we needed that half-hour break to absorb our loss.

Barb and I had booked vacation time after the tournament, so we wouldn't be returning home for another couple of weeks. We decided to skip the tournament's closing banquet. Otto Danieli, who was with one of the European teams, was driving to Garmisch-Partenkirchen, Germany, to watch the men's Worlds and he gave us a lift so we could go skiing there. Kay and Monica stayed behind because they were flying home the next day. What Barb and I didn't realize was that we were breaking a tradition of staying until the closing ceremonies. We hadn't understood the protocol. Maybe we just hadn't cared enough to ask. We should have known better, but we just wanted to get out of there. It was unheard of for anybody to walk away from the World Curling Championships before it officially ended—and this included the closing banquet—but we did. Later, Monica told us that we had missed the event of a lifetime. The banquet was held in a ritzy golf club that was like a palace and featured the finest service: multiple courses, special coffees, and, of course, Swiss chocolate.

We had a good time skiing, trying to get over our disappointment. It felt good to be active and somewhere that was just *away*. We returned home and didn't think anything of missing the banquet until a letter came in the mail a few weeks later. It was from the Canadian Curling Association, saying it was investigating why we left early. The World Curling Federation thought what we had done was unacceptable and we were being threatened with a one-year suspension. We'd caused a bit of an international incident, at least in the curling world.

It never occurred to us that we were doing anything that would warrant a suspension. I'd earned a bit of a reputation for going against tradition. Chewing gum on the ice and practising with a Walkman—even wearing it during the Worlds when things got really tough. Some of the things I did may have rubbed folks the wrong way, but I never realized it at the time. Our saving grace was that there was nothing in the rules about leaving the World Championships early. Barb, who had just graduated from law school, figured out there was nothing stating that a team is obligated to stay until the final banquet. We were let go with a reprimand, but that was definitely a scary time.

At home, it took awhile to get over losing—even today, it takes me awhile to mentally overcome a loss. I had become incredibly hard on myself. For about six weeks I just moped around. The ice had been removed from the Mayflower Curling Club because the season had ended, so I couldn't work on my game. All I could do was sit and stew about our performance. One good thing happened, though, that brought me out of my funk a little bit. Arnie Patterson, who ran a local radio station in Halifax, organized a one-game showdown at the Metro Centre between our team and the new men's Canadian championship team from Thunder Bay, skipped by Al ("The Iceman") Hackner. It was dubbed and advertised as the "Great Canadian Showdown" and the "Battle of the Sexes." I don't remember the score, only that it was a pretty lopsided affair and we were on the losing end. The local television station broadcast it live and about five thousand fans came out to watch us play. It was a cool experience, even though they blew us away.

LOSING AT WORLDS was tough, but as always I started looking ahead to the next season. There was no summer ice back then, but we all had a fitness routine. That seems pretty rudimentary compared to today's training methods. I was determined to make it back to the Nationals, and come October, once the ice was back in, every day at noon I'd pick up Barb, who was working, and take her to the Halifax Curling Club to practise over her lunch break. It became part of our routine. I would tell Barb, "When you don't practise, you don't play that well." I laugh when I'm reminded of it. There I was telling my big sister, the person who first took me to the Mayflower, what it takes to be a good curler. But again, here is where it helped to have my sisters as teammates. They understand me. And Barb knew what I was trying to do. She's told me that leadership in a work situation means being able to say things that people may not want to hear.

We were very focused and creatures of habit, going through the same routine at every event we played in. We made sure we had breakfast that included some protein every day. It's physically draining playing in a week-long tournament. For Barb and Monica it was especially hard, because as the lead and second they had to do the most sweeping, which can be exhausting. We made sure we went to sleep every night right after we got home from the evening draw. We used ice and heat to help us recover from the daily aches and pains. And we never drank any alcohol. We approached our training as any other athlete would, but at the time other teams weren't doing that. Remember, this was long before curling became an Olympic sport and long before the sport embraced real training.

Even with all of the training and work, we lost the next year in our own Provincials, which took place in Liverpool, Nova Scotia. In one of the games we lost, the opposing skip made a one-in-a-million shot through a very narrow port and somehow got a double takeout. Afterwards, I told the media that she'd never make that shot again in her life—and that's when I learned the golden rule of trying to lose gracefully. I'd made it sound like she'd fluked the shot and gotten totally lucky—and maybe she had—but I should have been more gracious. If you don't have anything nice to say, don't say anything at all.

After the 1983 season, I felt we needed to shake up the team to re-energize things. Monica and Barb stayed, but I replaced Kay Smith with Wendy Currie. This is something I did a lot of during my curling career, and it is so hard to make these changes. For starters, you become friends with your curling teammates, so cutting them is hard. But when something wasn't working, if the magic wasn't there, I always felt it was appropriate to bring in some fresh blood. Wendy Currie was a solid player who I had always admired and I thought she'd be a good addition.

The new team gelled quickly. We won every competition we entered in that 1984 season and then won the provincial championship. This meant we were going back to the Scott Tournament of Hearts. And, adding to the excitement for us, it was close to home, over in Charlottetown, Prince Edward Island.

In the opening game, we played Manitoba's Connie Laliberte, nicknamed "The Ice Queen" because she didn't show any emotion while curling. I first played against Connie in 1976 at the Canadian Junior Curling Championships in Thunder Bay. She was then playing second for Patti Vandekerckhove, and I was amazed by her talent. Connie—playing with her twin sister, Corinne; older sister Janet; and Chris More—would become one of the most dominant skips in Canada and the world. However, the 1984 Scott Tournament of Hearts was her first time skipping on the national stage. We beat Connie's team 6–4 in the round robin, but I had a feeling we would meet again in the playoffs.

Beginning in 1982, the Canadian Curling Association (CCA) started enforcing violations if a player did not clearly release his or her hand from the stone before crossing the hog line—a horizontal line about eleven feet in front of the house. The rule is that if there is a hog line violation, the rock is removed from play and the rocks on the sheet are returned to their original position. It's like playing with one less rock than the other team, and we repeatedly had rocks pulled because of hog line violations. Losing a rock changes the entire complexion of an end. Traditionally, the hog line rule was mostly observed using the honour system. We were all competitive, but curling has always been a very friendly and forthright game. Cheating was never tolerated. But, with the continuing growth of the game, the CCA brought in hog line judges to decide whether a player was going over the line. The problem was that they were placed in the gondola high above centre ice. It was from this skewed position that they were determining whether a player released the rock before crossing the hog line. I was having rocks pulled left, right, and centre, and after one game I was so angry I used the term *pissed off* in an interview with the media. I didn't mind having hog line judges, but their vantage point was wrong. They needed to be at ice level and on the line to make the proper call. But my choice of words set off a controversy in which CCA officials convened with Nova Scotia Curling Association reps Shirley Morash, Elsie Crosby, and Joyce Myers to determine whether I would be suspended. Fortunately, after their meeting, they decided not to suspend me. Instead, I was told (in more official words than these) to check my delivery regarding the point of release and to not make any more public statements about the issue to the media.

Beginning the following year, in 1985, the CCA decided to position the hog line judges in the dividers that separate the sheets, right on ice level. Even so, players became increasingly frustrated with hog line violations because it all came down to the accuracy of the judge, and human error is always a possibility. Like me, Randy Ferbey, who won six Canadian men's championships and four Worlds, had a lot of rocks pulled.

Today, there's a high-tech fix for hog lines. A Saskatoon-based company, Startco Engineering Ltd., devised technology to embed a sensor in every stone, which would determine whether or not a rock was clearly released. A flashing red light indicated a violation while a green light indicated no foul. The technology, which became known as Eye on the Hog, was introduced in December 2003 and is now used at all Canadian and World curling competitions. It removed the potential for human error. I like to think I had something to do with moving the hog line judges from high above centre ice to ice level at the hog lines. I can't take any credit for the electronics in the rocks, though.

After facing a second threat of suspension from the curling world, I gained a bit of a reputation as a rebel. This always struck me as funny, because it is so not my nature. Looking back on all of it, I don't think I was rebellious. I think I was simply oblivious to consequences because I was busy doing my own thing. I was an intense competitor. A lot of people who know me might be surprised by that intensity, but I became a different person on the ice compared to the way I act off of it. That part of me comes out only when I'm curling. It's a part of my personality that I discovered only because of the game, and I am very conscious of keeping it confined to that part of my life.

Despite the hog line rulings, and with the threat of suspension no longer hanging over me, we finished in first place after the round robin with a record of 9–1. Connie's team tied for second place with British Columbia's Lindsay Sparkes at 8–2, but because Connie's team had beaten Lindsay's in the round robin, they were placed second. Connie seemed like a machine to me in that tournament because she didn't miss much and was so strong. When Connie's team played Lindsay's to decide who would advance to the finals, Connie's team won in an extra end, by a score of 5–4.

The following day was the championship finals. I remember being really nervous about being back in the big game. There is something I should say about these finals: This was 1984, long before the three-rock and then four-rock rule came into being. Defence ruled the game then and it was hard to generate points. In any event, we jumped out to a 3–1 lead after three ends, and Connie played conservatively through the next three ends, saving her last-rock advantage. Then she seized an opportunity in the seventh end and scored three. We blanked the next two ends, so we could have last rock coming home. And here is where the four-rock rule would have made a big difference, as it was hard to set up corner guards, to set up the two points we needed to win. So we only scored one to tie the game, forcing an extra end.

Meanwhile, even though the game was going into an extra end, the bagpipers began playing, thinking it was over. Nobody had told them there was such a thing as extra ends in curling. I remember chuckling as the officials went over to the bagpipers to give them the "cut" signal. Once the piping stopped, we settled in to play the extra end, looking for a steal and the win. On skip's rocks, Connie made an amazing shot with her first rock, coming around a stone in front and landing on top of the button. I needed to make an even better shot: follow her down and push her stone back just a bit. I let the rock go, and the sweepers backed off it. But then halfway down the ice it picked up some debris—the curling terminology is a "pick"—and went sideways, failing to come anywhere close to what I had planned. Just like that, we lost. The rock basically died. You see a lot of picks in curling, but I had never seen one that lost a Canadian finals. Connie didn't even have to throw her last rock.

When my son Luke saw footage of it years later, he said there was no way it was going to curl around the stone in front anyway (thanks, Luke). But it hadn't even got to that magical spot, six feet before the hog line, when it would gradually start to curl. Losing on a pick is just plain hard; there are so many "what ifs?" I was angry and disappointed, and not happy with the curling gods. Did I cry? No. I did what I always do: I stewed and lost sleep and that bout probably lasted a week. With a pick, it's harder to analyze what you could have done differently. But that didn't stop me from trying. Still, I admired and respected Connie. Her win that day began what would be a great curling career. She would go on to prevail in the World Championships that year and win additional Canadian women's titles in 1992 and 1995 in her Hall of Fame career. As an aside, Connie's 1984 team and my 1982 team are the only three-sister combinations to win the Canadian championship. I have always been such a big Connie fan. We all have idols in the sport, and she was mine.

I'd come so close to winning the Nationals again—just one shot away. That's exactly what you dream of as a competitor: winning the day when everything is riding on you. That pressure was why I always had to skip: I wanted so much to be in that position. What I didn't know after losing to Connie was that it was going to take a long time to get that close again. My personal and professional lives were about to take precedence over my curling career.

CHAPTER 5
OFF THE ICE

Through the late 1970s and early 1980s, there was a lot happening for me. I was competing and travelling for the first time, but I was also young and exploring life. However, as I always say, everything I have in my life is because of curling—right down to my husband, Scott. I met him through our mutual love of the game. In 2015, we celebrated thirty-two years of marriage.

In our house we nickname him Spock, because he's very logical and has a solution to everything, presented in a calm and reasonable way. He's very much the strong, silent type, and so my polar opposite, really. He is from a curling family, and I first noticed him during our junior curling days when I was just sixteen. He was over on another sheet. I thought he was kind of cute, and still do!

We had our first date in 1979. We went to see *Star Trek: The Motion Picture*, as it had just come out (this could be where the Spock nickname came from). We've always been a good fit with great chemistry, and it helped that he was just as passionate about curling. When it came to competitive curling, my mood shifted from really high to very low after a bad loss. Scott always helped to bring me around. He knew when I was down that it would pass, so he didn't get all worked up about me being upset over losses. He was really supportive of my whole curling career. We both understood losses and each other's mindset. He understood the work and energy that went into trying to be great, and he supported my journey at every step.

Having a curling partner helped our relationship develop. It was nice to have something we could do together and share. But he helped my curling. Scott was a great sounding board for ideas and thoughts about the game, and he became the biggest factor in my curling life. Even before we started dating in the late 1970s, we used to go to the Halifax Curling Club and throw rocks together. Then we'd have lunch and throw more rocks. We played games against each other a lot and I think he dreaded it, because I wouldn't leave the ice until I'd won the game. I'd be so mad if he beat me, and because he was such a good player I had to keep improving in order to win our one-on-one battles. It definitely made me a better player.

Scott also went to Dalhousie University, but unlike me he focused on studying and completed his degree in Science and Mechanical Engineering. He played in two Canadian Junior Curling Championships and was runner-up in 1978.

While my own career was ramping up, in 1980 I played third for Scott in the Canadian Mixed Curling Championship. Years later, in 1993, we'd win that Canadian title. While we played together for years, we eventually stopped because it was too hard to squeeze into our already busy personal and professional schedules.

As mentioned, I had done some sports reporting during the World Championships I played in, but professionally my career as a broadcaster began in the summer of 1982. I was playing in a softball game against members of the media. I was not a softball player, but I got a call to come and play anyway. It was totally random, yet one of those moments I just said "yes" to, almost as if the universe was dragging me along. Saying "yes" that day wound up leading to a job! Chuck Bridges, the news director at CJCH, approached me afterwards and asked if I had ever thought of working in the media. When I had done those daily phone interviews with CJOH during the 1982 Worlds, Chuck felt it gave listeners an idea of what the competition was like from an athlete's point of view as opposed to hearing it from a reporter. He thought it was time to bring on a sportscaster who lived the life of an international-calibre athlete. This was a bit of serendipity, because I had always wanted to be a reporter. My grade seven teacher, Miss McKinnon, told me I'd be good at it because I was always asking questions. Maybe she was psychic.

Chuck gave me his business card and I called him the following day to audition for a weekend sports reporter's job at CJCH. The audition didn't go so great, but Paul Mennier, who was in the sound booth with me, encouraged me to keep doing another take—and another, and another. I was "overenunciating," something that is common among people starting out in broadcasting. I also had a very nasal sound. A lot of people, when they hear their voice for the first time, say the same thing: "Is that really what I sound like?" As well, I sounded very monotone. So far, these were many strikes against a radio career.

Anyhow, I probably did a hundred takes of the copy (I'm not exaggerating), and each time I would adjust something about the read. With Paul's suggestions and encouragement, we finally got one that sounded not half bad and was mistake free. We slid the reel under Chuck's door, and then I waited. He called the next day, said he liked what he heard, and offered me an intern spot. I was ecstatic from day one. I wasn't getting paid, and the shift started at 4 a.m., but I couldn't have loved it more. I had found my calling. And to think it all began by saying "yes" to a softball game.

As soon as I got in the newsroom, I was a sponge. I just loved it. I loved talking to people, I loved reporting. I loved everything about it. After working the whole summer for free, I finally got a one-year contract. I still have a copy of that first contract, with the huge (for that time) $14,000 per year earnings. I felt super lucky. I worked with John Gallagher at the time and watched how he broadcasted sports, wrote scripts, and phoned contacts.

After a while, once I'd grown in confidence and the station had grown more confident in me, I started to go on the air. In those days, reporters would also cover sports events, so I spent a lot of time in and out of locker rooms. Back then, not a lot of women were doing that sort of thing. Because of my own curling career, I felt I knew what was going on in the minds of athletes, and I wanted to do whatever I could to share that perspective. More than anything, I respected the athletes and understood the work they put into their sport and the sacrifices they made on their journeys. Most knew who I was, and I found they would talk to me in ways they wouldn't to other sportscasters. I never found that being a woman in a male-dominated position was a problem for me. I just did the job as best I could and the response was very positive. Now there are plenty of female sports reporters, but back in the early 1980s it was still a novelty.

Ultimately, I loved telling stories. I was always enthusiastic about whatever I was reporting on, and I think people responded to that—whether it was the athletes I was interviewing or the people listening in. I think athletes are very hard on themselves—I certainly always was—and I tried to get people to open up about how they had performed.

My first big interview happened in 1983 when I was assigned a story on Ken Dryden. Not only had he been the Montreal Canadiens' star goalie, but he had also played for Team Canada in the 1972 Summit Series against the Soviet Union. He was, and still is, one of Canada's most famous athletes. Dryden's seminal hockey book, *The Game*, had just been published and he was doing a media tour. I booked an interview for the current affairs show *Nova Scotia Today*, which used to air on C100. The interview took place in the backyard of a representative from the book's publisher. I couldn't have been more excited, because it was huge to have an opportunity to interview one of the greatest goalies in National Hockey League history. I read Dryden's book to prepare, loved it, and marvelled at the similarities between a goalie and a skip. Sure, he played for a legendary team and I was a curler, but as my broadcasting career continued and I interviewed more athletes from a variety of sports I realized that all athletes have so much in common: dedication, relentless practice, hard losses, huge wins, and single-mindedness. Every athlete knows what it's like to walk that path.

So, going into that interview, I felt like I understood his journey. Mind you, few athletes have been able to write such a classic memoir so eloquently. Ken Dryden was one of my first interviews, and one of my favourites. It was also perhaps the longest. I must have used both sides of a sixty-minute cassette tape. Between my having five hundred questions and Dryden known for being verbose, the interview went on far longer than I think either of us had expected. I had to take a razor blade to it once I got into editing. I had a hundred and twenty minutes of tape, for a four-minute segment. I learned a valuable lesson about the importance of focusing an interview and being judicious and smart. Whenever I conduct a too-long interview now, I think back to 1983 and say to myself, "I'm pulling a Dryden again." Dryden is actually hard to edit down, because everything that comes out of his mouth is eloquent and brilliant. Years later, I told him this story when I saw him again. He was very good at pretending to remember the interview (let's face it, he's done thousands), and chuckled when I told him it took me forever to edit him down.

In many ways, growing up in a big family helped prepare me for life as a reporter. In the Jones house, we needed to know how to tell a good story—with a beginning, a middle, and an end—around the dinner table. If a story was boring, someone would tell you so. But if a story was good, you owned the table. Radio reminded me of dinner-table conversation: an intimate conversation between the host and the listener.

I was lucky to have worked with and learned from amazing people in the industry. Steve Murphy, the late Dave Wright, Joanne Clancy, Rick Howe, Gerry Fogarty, Chuck Bridges, and Pat Connolly were all guides in the early days. Later, there were the late Don Wittman and Geoff Gowan, Henry Champ, Bill Cameron, and Heather Hiscox. I learned from everyone I worked with, but these wonderful journalists all gave me a helping hand. I watched, listened, and emulated them. With my new job, I started a juggling act. I was now a full-time worker while training for the sport I loved. Unlike during university, I was determined to manage my time better. I started learning how to dance while juggling.

Things were going well at the station, and I think they were pleased by the audience reception. They gave me a new assignment: In 1983, I started covering Nova Scotia Voyageurs hockey games at the Metro Centre for radio. They were the American Hockey League farm team for the Montreal Canadiens. The Voyageurs were almost the exclusive domain of men. Marilla Stephenson was covering the Voyageurs for *The Chronicle Herald*, so I wasn't the only female. And before us, Gail Rice had covered the Voyageurs and also done play-by-play.

This brings us to the locker room issue. I hated reporting from the locker room, for several reasons. I didn't like people coming into my locker room when I was competing; reporters waited for us to come out instead. So, why should I go into the Voyageurs locker room? Do athletes give their best interviews while sweaty, wrapped in a towel, or naked? I went to the team's media rep and said I'd prefer that the players I needed to talk to be brought out to me. They agreed, and that worked well.

I don't think you get a lot of insight from a locker room interview. It's supposed to be quick and easy access for reporters working to a deadline. We all did it because it was part of the job and the tradition of sports reporting. But I found I would get better clips when it was a one-on-one situation and everybody was in a relaxed atmosphere. I never had any players be rude or obnoxious to me because I was a woman, but I've heard about it happening to other women in the dressing room. The players always treated me with respect, though, in or out of that room. Maybe it was because in Nova Scotia they knew me as both a reporter and an athlete. They knew I was a curler; I was not an unknown face to them. I think that helped. Things have changed a lot on the locker room front. When I've covered NHL games, Memorial Cups, or Ice Hockey World Junior Championships, they bring players out in front of the team or event's signage. For Stanley Cup playoffs, they have a big interview room. And at the Olympics, they parade everyone through a cordoned-off area.

Because I have competed in national and international sporting events, I have empathy for athletes when I'm interviewing them. Throughout my life I've encountered reporters who have been totally unsympathetic while interviewing an athlete who has just experienced something emotionally upsetting. Sometimes a reporter just needs a quick quote, and doesn't care that an athlete has put in all sorts of time, effort, sweat, and everything else. The reporter has a deadline and needs as much raw emotion as possible. Often, a question is asked that shows no sensitivity to the situation. If someone has just experienced a horrific game or moment, no matter what the event, my inner reaction is always *I'm so sorry.* I feel for them. Every time I watch a person lose, I feel myself losing again. I think when you can bring empathy to a story, you end up getting more out of the person being interviewed. I've walked a mile in these athletes' shoes. It might be a totally different sport, but each one of us has the exact same story: one of sacrifice and hard work. You give up a lot of yourself and your time to play a sport at a competitive level. Yes, there are rewards, but chasing that championship comes at a price. As a curler, I hate getting clichéd questions. It's hard not to answer a clichéd question with a clichéd answer. I grew up listening to the Royal Canadian Air Farce and hearing Big Bobby Clobber say, "I put the puck in the net" when asked how he scored. A lot of sports interviews never get past that point, and as a reporter I try to focus my interviews to get something more.

THROUGHOUT THIS PERIOD, one thing was clear. No matter how things were going at the station and in my curling career, Scott and I were growing closer. We were still in that wonderful new-love stage when, on my birthday in 1983, he proposed. We had been together since 1980, and hadn't really discussed marriage. But why discuss it when you know you're with your soul mate? We planned for a June 29, 1984, wedding date, and when I say "planned" I use the word loosely. These were the 1980s, before anyone had heard of a wedding planner. I bought my wedding dress at the famous store Filene's Basement in Boston while on the road covering the Nova Scotia Voyageurs during their run for the Calder Cup. I think I paid fifty bucks for the dress. We kept things nice and simple. We married just down the street from the house I grew up in, at St. Agnes Church. My sisters Barb and Monica were my maids of honour, and Scott's brothers Kent and Bruce were his best men. A bagpiper played a curling tune outside the church. It was a big, but simple wedding. The reception was at the Halifax Curling Club. We went to beautiful St. Andrews, New Brunswick, for a honeymoon at the Algonquin Resort; it's still our favourite place to go.

As soon as I got home from the honeymoon, I started my job as a TV broadcaster, beginning at ATV. I thought I was just about the luckiest person on the planet. This was during the time cable TV was launching, and in Halifax I think there were still only six channels. It's laughable now to think of this—everybody was talking about the death of radio. In fact, radio has never been stronger, but in 1984 the fear was that this thing called cable television was exploding and nobody was going to listen to radio anymore. I bought into that fear too, so thought I'd better get in on the whole cable thing and figure out how to do TV. Today, online news and entertainment is exploding and many wonder about the future of TV. It's not the first time I've heard the doom-and-gloom reports. ATV was attached to the radio building, which was convenient. Mind you, we had to crawl through a half basement to get between the two, but we were still attached. I knew the television people well, and when the late-night sports reporter job came open, I auditioned. Once again, much like my radio audition two years earlier, I did multiple takes before getting one that was halfway decent. I did look a bit like a deer caught in the headlights—I had not yet perfected the art of the "anchor look-away"—but they saw some potential there and hired me anyway.

I was definitely fascinated by the television industry. Throughout my life, I've been a student of everything I've done. When I decide I'm going to do something, I coach myself, find mentors, and get others to help guide or teach me. I listened well and I was hard on myself—but not in the way I was after a tough curling loss. Instead of beating myself up, my attitude was more like, *I did it, now how can I improve and do it better?* So I studied myself on videotape and studied other people's work and was not afraid to ask questions about how to improve my broadcasting skills. I had often asked people questions or sought advice on curling, and applied that same approach to television. I asked for help from everybody in the business who I admired. Perhaps my strength in both curling and broadcasting is that I've always been smart enough to know what I don't know and determined enough to find the people who can give me the answers.

Being a TV broadcaster is much different than being a radio broadcaster. Radio's strength is that it creates a very personal experience with whoever is listening, with only a voice and the story. I love that. Television, on the other hand, is the opposite. I thought it would be an easy transition, but with that huge camera and the big lights ... what a change from radio.

I did sports stories for the show *Live at 5*, hosted by Dave Wright, which had shockingly high ratings. The show, a news program, coined the expression "Maritime neighbourhood." And it was broadcast throughout Nova Scotia, New Brunswick, and Prince Edward Island. It was conversational in tone and its set was very inviting, like stepping into someone's living room to hear what you needed to know. I was also hosting sports at midnight on the late-night news. Again, in 1984, women hosting sports broadcasts was still pretty rare. I was slowly getting the hang of it all, but it seemed like life was moving along at warp speed. Then, everything changed again. Zach, our first son, entered our world in the summer of 1986 and life got even better. It was wonderful. I'd always heard that giving birth is a miracle, and it's true. It was a surreal moment, realizing that my life had changed forever. Suddenly, it wasn't just me and Scott anymore, and we were responsible for this tiny person. It was the most beautiful moment of our lives. We felt the same way when Luke was born seven years later, like life was fresh all over again. I always look at them both as absolute miracles. These perfect little people came from me, and that blows my mind. I never take it for granted. I've always thought it was the most special, beautiful thing Scott and I could ever do.

I have always been comfortable around lots of kids. Because I was one of nine children, I grew up helping out with babies. But because my mother made raising nine kids look easy, I may have been a tad naive about motherhood while I was pregnant. I never thought that being a working mother was going to be hard, but going to work after a sleepless night is never easy. Luckily, Zach and Luke were awesome babies. As our kids grew up, Scott and I got used to juggling schedules: hockey, tennis, and homework for the kids and our own work and curling. With both Zach and Luke playing rep hockey, our fridge calendar was crazy busy. But our boys were flexible and adaptable, too. They'd often come with me when I had to do interviews at night, and even made trips with me to the Olympics and Commonwealth Games in the 1990s. They were great as kids and both have grown to be amazing men. They are thoughtful, kind, and smart, but I know I'm just a tiny bit biased.

There was always so much going on that I got pretty good at juggling. I had a lot of energy, and I made systems for doing things. I had a system just for cooking: On Sunday, I'd make a meal for that night and four other meals for the rest of the week. Beef stew, lasagna, and sweet and sour chicken were our staples. That way I didn't have to come home after work and cook dinner. Dinner was always there; mind you, we all have a bit of an aversion to leftovers now.

Even though we had only two kids, that fridge calendar had us all moving constantly. Almost all of our activities involved ice or dry-land training. Yes, the boys had other things going on, like music lessons, but come 6 p.m., it wasn't unusual for us to be at Centennial Arena all night, starting with Luke's novice hockey practice, followed by Zach's bantam practice. Luke used to come to the curling club with me and throw rocks while I threw on the next sheet over. Although he focused on tennis, he dabbled in curling and had enough talent to play on the Nova Scotia team that went to the Canadian Junior Curling Championships in 2013. Both Zach and Luke competed in the Canada Games—Zach in hockey (with Sidney Crosby) and Luke in tennis—and both inherited a love of fitness and exercise that hopefully will stay with them until they are one hundred years old.

If I had started a family too early in life, my curling game might never have developed the way it did. Everybody does what's best for them. We added children to the mix while I was working on my broadcasting career and constantly training and competing, and I couldn't have managed without the support of a spouse that has my back at every turn. I certainly have that with Scott. I had already won a Canadian championship before we married. He knew what he was buying into, and he supported me through everything. But it is sort of funny: We planned nothing, really, but everything fell perfectly into place as if we'd had a plan.

I HAD BEEN working at ATV for about two years when a job opened up at CBC just down the street. Don Martin, a long-time CBC sportscaster, was heading to a big sportscasting job in Toronto. So I applied and got an audition. I was so excited when I got this job, and felt very lucky. It was the same job I'd been doing at ATV, but it was for the supper-hour broadcast. Everyone dreamed of working at CBC (and I'm sure they still do). I began my brand new job at CBC two weeks after Zach's birth. Yeah, I know that's crazy. And throw in chaotic. But that's how life goes.

Scott had been working as a subsea engineer in the oil patch off of Newfoundland. He had a three-weeks-on, three-weeks-off schedule and we decided with a baby on the way and the career opportunity for me at CBC, it would be best if I took the job and he left the oil rig life. If Scott and I had ever had a master plan, maybe we would have planned a baby and career differently. But we weren't those kinds of people. We are more like my blueberry crisp recipe: Just throw it all together almost any which way and it all turns out good in the end.

My new job at CBC was specifically for the supper-hour show *1st Edition*. It's hard to imagine now, with twenty-four-hour news and continual online updates, but back in 1986 the first opportunity to hear the news after that morning's paper was at suppertime. The show followed a typical supper-hour news format that really hasn't changed much over the years. There was local news first, then international news, followed by weather and sports. I put together the highlights for the NHL, NFL, NBA, and MLB, depending on the season. These all came in on news feeds, cut into four-minute highlight packs. From there I would cut them down even further to fit into our four-minute (total) sportscast. I would also shoot a local human-interest sports story. That could be on the high school football team looking to win a fifth straight championship or on someone like Stephen Giles, a sprint canoeist, training for the Olympic Games.

I love reporting on all kinds of things, but I was always drawn to sports broadcasting. In 1987, a year after starting at CBC, I was assigned to the national curling beat as a colour analyst for the Brier and Scotties tournaments. Joan Mead, who worked as the executive producer for the curling broadcasts, wanted me to be part of the coverage. She was considered to be a very innovative producer and was extremely supportive of my curling and broadcasting. As soon as she'd learn that I was curling for Nova Scotia in the Scotties, she'd say, "I hope you win, but if you don't, bring your on-air clothes and we'll put you to work." Joan was also a real mentor for female broadcasters, pushing me to be better.

While Joan produced a lot of sports, her contribution to curling was huge. Certainly, Joan did a lot to advance the sport on television. She was always trying out new shooting styles and graphics, and she strongly argued for the need to mic all of the players so they could tell their own stories. She passed away in 2000, but her legacy continues. To this day, her role in curling is recognized and honoured with the Joan Mead Builder Award, given each year to a person who has contributed to the growth of the women's game.

With curling, Joan was always trying to do the broadcasting part differently and better. She wanted to take curling to a new level, and I think bringing me on to do colour analysis was part of that. It was a new dynamic. I was a broadcaster but also a successful player, and she wanted me to join Don Duguid and Don Wittman and spice things up.

During my time on the curling broadcasting team, I learned a lot, and not just from Joan. It was a thrill to get that CBC Sports peach jacket and be on a team with the two Dons. Don Wittman was simply the best sports broadcaster around. He was Mr. Versatile and good at every sport he covered, whether it was hockey, football, or curling. And, of course, I adored Don's work with the late Geoff Gowan, who was CBC's analyst for track and field.

Don Duguid is a Curling Hall of Fame legend from Manitoba who won three Brier championships and two World Championships. He is an institution in Canadian curling. One of his favourite phrases when it comes to discussing strategy is "there's two schools of thought." There were times when Don would discuss the strategy happening on the ice and I would say something like, "Yeah, but you could also play this shot." When that happened, some people thought I was criticizing Don. An article written by legendary curling broadcaster Bill Good essentially said, *Oh, the nerve of her, criticizing Don Duguid.* Robin Wilson, the coordinator of the Scotties, said she received numerous emails from viewers wondering why Don and I were always arguing, and asking why didn't I keep quiet and let him talk. But Arthur Smith, the head of CBC Sports at the time, loved it. He said that having one person say one thing and another say something else was exactly what audiences were doing in their own homes while watching the game. And Joan Mead loved our back-and-forth analysis, so she encouraged us to keep our style. Don and I were surprised when we'd hear people say that we didn't get along. We adored one another and had so much fun together. When I would suggest different shots on air, some people didn't like it. But viewership kept growing. I guess it all just proves Don's "two schools of thought."

Hindsight is a beautiful thing. While I enjoyed working with Witt and Duguid, covering the games was a bit detrimental to my own curling for all kinds of reasons. While I loved being a broadcaster, it took my mind away from competing. If we didn't make the playoffs at the Scotties, I would switch right over into broadcasting mode to report on the end of the tournament. Changing gears like that happened a lot. Mind you, my teams during that period were a notch below making it to the playoffs, but having a split focus is never a good thing. You need to be all in with whatever you're doing.

On the other hand, working on the CBC curling broadcast did help my game in many ways. I learned a lot about curling by being on the ice level with the CBC, watching the players, and going through everything with them. From there, I could listen to conversations and see body language that the viewers at home weren't seeing. It was a different way of experiencing the intense emotions I was used to seeing in competition, and I learned to sense when a turning point was about to happen. I took this different perspective with me into competitions and it benefited my curling, being down there watching the subtleties, nuances, and momentum shifts. I could almost predict who was going to win a game based on their body language. Even how a player walked into the arena seemed to signal something significant.

It was an exciting time, and there were a lot of changes coming for the game. Curling had debuted as a demonstration sport in the 1988 Winter Olympics in Calgary. That means it was not a full medal event, but rather a sport featured for the International Olympic Committee to decide if they would like to include it in future Olympics. A test run, so to speak. Since CTV had the broadcast rights to the Olympics that year, I didn't attend as a broadcaster, but naturally I was keenly interested. The Canadian Curling Association held two Olympic Trials Selection Camps—one in Eastern Canada at the Mississauga Country Club and the other in Western Canada at the Shamrock Curling Club in Edmonton—and chose forty men's and women's players from each region. Some players were chosen based on their recent accomplishments, while others were given an opportunity to attend the camps based on their curling performance in the previous three years. I was invited along with my sisters Monica and Barb. Each curler was tested individually on shot execution, sweeping, strategy, physical fitness, and psychological testing. I had never taken part in anything like that before, where I was being judged and scored as an individual. The curling tradition had always been four teammates winning on the ice in a game. Following the camps, five camp head coaches and two CCA board members convened to form four men's teams and four women's teams—all-star teams, if you will. I was selected, but Monica and Barb didn't make the cut. I was put on a team with Kay Zinck, Cathy Caudle, and Kim Dolan. With the teams already chosen, we headed to the first-ever Canadian Olympic Curling Trials, which took place in April 1987 in Calgary.

My team finished with a 4–3 record—not good enough to qualify for the playoffs. Vancouver's Linda Moore, who won the 1985 Scott Tournament of Hearts, won the women's division, while Calgary's Ed Lukowich, the 1986 Canadian and World champion, won the men's division. So, they represented Canada at the Calgary Olympics. Looking back, the whole process was a bit surreal. Being chosen as an individual felt odd at the time, and I think we had only four practices as a team before the actual Trials. Because curling's inclusion in the Olympics still wasn't a done deal, believe it or not, the Trials weren't a disappointing event to lose. In the late 1980s, the pinnacle was still to win the Brier or the Scotties. However, once curling became a full medal sport in 1998, it would change the face of the game in a profound way. But we didn't know how big a change that would be at those first Olympic Trials in 1987.

Curling was growing in a big way and in the late 1980s TSN moved into covering the sport. It covered the round robin of the Scotties and the Brier and then CBC would come in for the playoffs. This was done for several reasons. Not everyone had cable television, so keeping curling on a main network like CBC made sense. Also, no one knew what kind of ratings curling would draw on TSN during weekday coverage. Would wall-to-wall coverage on a still fairly new cable sports channel work? TSN President Jim Thompson, a former CBC executive, absolutely believed that curling would be a huge hit on cable. The way ratings are climbing today, it's hard to appreciate that TSN's commitment to curling was a bit of a gamble at the time. CBC also covered the Canadian junior tournaments, the Brier and Scotties, the two Worlds, and the Olympic Trials. It might not seem like a lot now, when there are hundreds of hours of curling coverage, but back then it was a lot of competition to cover in a short period of time.

The schedule was hard on reporters, too. With the majority of events held in Alberta, Saskatchewan, and Manitoba, it was a lot of travel. Plus, there were no online tools then to help close the distance between you and your family. But even if they'd had things like Skype or FaceTime then, I wouldn't have wanted to be a virtual mother. The travelling was wearing on me pretty quickly. I wanted to be home for the boys' hockey games, reading bedtime stories, making my chocolate chip cookies for them, and being part of whatever was happening at the time. Scott was supportive and terrific, but the road was not where I wanted to be.

Work–life balance is always a delicate teeter-totter. Instinctively, I knew I was compromising that balance every time I took a Sunday red-eye from the west to get home in time to groggily get my boys off to school on a Monday morning. Was that the kind of mother I wanted to be? Days before I was supposed to cover the Olympic Trials in 1997, I got a sign that this couldn't go on any longer. A babysitter cancelled on us. This seems like a relatively small thing, but it caused such a big problem! There was no way I could make the red-eye flight, and all the dominoes fell over. I phoned Joan Mead and told her I was done with weekend curling coverage. My strength has always been compartmentalizing family, work, and curling into separate boxes. The trick is to never squeeze too much into each of those boxes. Giving up covering curling, as much as I enjoyed it, helped me to keep the lid on other things. I have high energy, but maintaining that high energy means recognizing when the lid is on too tight. I was still a full-time CBC employee, but dropping the weekend curling coverage from my schedule and saying goodbye to red-eye flights opened a big door in my own curling life. You know what they say: When one door closes, another opens. That old saying was about to be proven very true.

CHAPTER 6
BUILDING BLOCKS

I had been curling competitively for years, but the ultimate goal had eluded me: winning the Canadian women's championship and finishing it off with a victory at the Worlds. As much as I loved reporting and travelling, I was aching to win another Canadian championship. I'd been working to improve my game and the teams I'd put together had represented Nova Scotia proudly, but the pieces were never all there. To win, it's a matter of finding the right combination of talented players; it's called chemistry, and you can't win without it. I had Nancy Delahunt and Kim Kelly with me for most of the 1990s, and I knew they were world-class curlers. We found the final ingredient when Mary-Anne Arsenault agreed to join our team in the spring of 1997. She was the missing piece of the puzzle.

The pool of players is small in Nova Scotia compared to other provinces like Alberta and Manitoba; there are only so many to choose from to build a winning team. Throughout the 1990s, my teams qualified several times to represent

Nova Scotia in the Scott Tournament of Hearts, but each time we fell short of making the playoffs. Don Duguid and Don Wittman used to call me "six and five," because I went to the Scotties so many times and always ended up with a 6–5 record or close to that, never quite breaking through. But we always knew in our hearts that we were so close to the top rinks, and that we lost some games by an inch, which just as easily could have been wins with a break along the way.

So each year, thanks to being a very stubborn person, I stuck with it, and through the lean years I kept working to find the players who would meld into a cohesive unit. In curling at the national level, both men's and women's, there are always four solid teams that can win the event and then there are several teams at that .500 mark that are a player or two away from being great. My teams worked hard and plugged away. Yes, we were a little discouraged at times, but we weren't throwing in the towel. We always thought the talent was there.

At the start of every Scotties, hope springs eternal. All of the competitors think they're going to win it. When we'd lose by just an inch, ending with our 6–5 or 5–6 record, I was always shocked. Not once did I think that people were saying, "Yes, she's making it to the tournament, but she's not winning." But maybe, after several years, that was exactly what people had come to expect. Competitors have to have really tough skin. We all like winning, but we also know that losing is a possibility. Above all, competitors learn the very useful life skill of picking themselves back up and playing harder the next time. I know that's such a cliché, but it's the most important part of becoming a champion. As a player and reporter, I learned to not spend my life thinking about what other people are saying or what reporters are writing.

You simply can't let it enter your headspace. I think curling fans knew we were fighting in every game, so I never felt I was being judged for having won the Nationals only once. If I had heard anything negative, I know I would have been able to ignore it. It's a choice to ignore it and maintain a single-minded approach to competing. The world is full of negativity; if you're doing what you love, you can't pay any attention to the naysayers.

My teams had a hard road and went through tough losses, year after year. But when Kim, Mary-Anne, Nancy, and I finally got together, we knew we had a bit of magic in us. Kim had played as my fifth (the alternate) beginning in the late 1980s and joined the lineup in 1991, throwing second stone. The role of the alternate is a bit of a thankless one. She travels to the Nationals with the team so she can be ready to play in case someone is injured or falls sick. Kim never actually got to play as an alternate, but I knew she had great talent and she is the feistiest competitor. I saw glimmers of greatness in her, and was motivated to keep her on my teams. She started at second in the 1980s, but when she moved to third in 1999 it really changed the dynamic of the team. Kim is fierce on the ice, like a dog with a bone when it comes to competing—that girl hates to lose even more than I do. She was so determined in that third spot and made a lot of shots. Double takeouts, tap backs, and gorgeous hit and rolls. She created extra points with some killer shots. I had played with other good thirds before Kim, and she had been a great second, but the answer had been right in front of our eyes. Once I had the idea of moving her to third, it took some convincing. She had been a lifelong front-end player (playing lead or second stone). We talked around her kitchen table and got her to give it a try. It was a perfect fit.

Mary-Anne was another secret weapon. She first played for me in 1993 as lead and became pivotal for our team as second. Mary-Anne is very calm and a natural hitter, so second was a great position for her on our team. She had played third for Heather Rankin and they got close to winning the Provincials. When Heather left the province for Alberta, Mary-Anne started skipping her own team. I think her attitude about joining our team was "If I can't beat them, join them." We were lucky she did.

Nancy was our alternate in 1991 and became a regular part of my team in 1996. Nancy and I go way back: We competed against each other as high school curlers when she played for Windsor and I played for St. Patrick's High School. She is not just an amazing player; her ability to see the good in everything is such an asset.

We all had qualities that blended well. Nancy was the eternal optimist on the team—a cup-half-full kind of person. We joke that she sees the world through rose-coloured glasses, and that's a very good thing. She's also really bright on the ice about seeing options and strategy. Sometimes we'd all be looking at one shot and it would be Nancy who would say, "Have you thought about this?" And she was always right. Nancy, Kim, and I are very talkative and boisterous, so that meshed well, and Mary-Anne's calm, positive energy became really important. Mary-Anne didn't talk much on the ice, but when she did we all listened. Nancy was the vice-skip, even though she threw lead stones. She would come into the house and hold the broom for me, to provide the line for my shots. Normally, the player who throws third stone holds the broom for the skip, but in our case it worked well to have the lead do it. Nancy jokes that she had a "big-ass attitude" about strategy; she certainly helped me to read the ice, and because I trusted her she became a good sounding board for me to bounce around ideas.

We knew we were really good from the start of the 1998–1999 season. I remember we played in a cashspiel in Thunder Bay in November. It was a great field and we were really dominant. We were just a comfortable foursome. We looked at each other and knew there was something special about our squad. Our team kept building and getting better as the season progressed into the provincial playdowns. Kim had a specific moment in her family room at home before leaving for the Scotties that year. She was thinking we were ready to win because of the way we had played throughout the season. A similar moment happened at my home, too. My husband talked to me before we left for the Scotties and he said, "Don't be afraid to actually assert yourself and win some games, because this team is good enough to do it." He was telling me to have confidence. We all believed.

The 1999 Scotties took place in Charlottetown, which was almost like playing at home since Prince Edward Island is so close to Halifax. Kim had a premonition during the opening ceremonies that we were going to win. It was a feeling of being ready. But while we were feeling good about our chances, we were still an underdog team. The field was headed by the reigning champions from Alberta, skipped by Cathy King (her last name had been Borst when she'd won), and included teams skipped by former Canadian or world champions such as Pat Sanders of British Columbia, Connie Laliberte of Manitoba, and Kim Gellard of Ontario. Maybe we were considered underdogs because people had gotten used to writing us off. Maybe they were thinking, *Here comes the 6–5 team again.*

I was asked by the organizing committee to give the opening speech during the banquet that kicks off the competition.

This is usually reserved for a person who has retired from the game, someone who gets up and speaks about their glory days. I remember thinking at the time, *They must think I'm not going to do well in the tournament, so I may as well be the guest speaker.* The event began the following day, and we started off on the right foot. We opened with an 8–5 win over B.C., followed by a tight 3–2 victory over Alberta. We continued with wins over New Brunswick and Northwest Territories/ Yukon and then faced Cathy King's Team Canada. Beginning in 1985, the Canadian Curling Association and Scott Paper gave the reigning winner an automatic entry to the tournament the following year without them having to go through the provincial qualifying process.

I had played Cathy many times in my career, going back to juniors, so there was a lot of history between us and I really admired her. My team started off strongly with two points in the second end and led 7–1 after five, which I think was a big surprise to everyone watching. After we scored four in the seventh to lead 11–3, Cathy decided to shake hands and concede. We continued to roll along with wins over P.E.I., Saskatchewan, and Quebec, improving to an 8–0 record. Then we played Manitoba, which had a 4–3 record and was skipped by Connie Laliberte, another of my long-time competitors since juniors. We lost that game 5–2, and then lost our next two games against Newfoundland/Labrador and Ontario. As a result, we finished the round robin tied with Manitoba at 8–3. But we were exactly where we wanted to be: playoff bound. It felt so good to be in the thick of the race.

Although we had the same record, Manitoba was placed ahead of us because we had lost to them in the round robin. We played each another in the opening round of the playoffs in the one-two game. The playoff format is that the top two teams battle and the winner advances to the finals. The loser is guaranteed a spot in the semifinals, facing the winner of the playoff game between the third- and fourth-place teams for another chance to get to the final game. Only Connie's Manitoba team was intimidating to me, because I had such respect for her. I had known Connie for so much of my career, and she was always a rock-solid competitor. It wasn't just her delivery, but also her calm demeanour. Since beating me at the Scotties in 1984, she had won two Canadian titles and placed second in another. To me, Connie was a machine.

We always believed in man-to-man defence—in outplaying the opponent at each position—and I knew I had to take care of Connie. That was my challenge, to be the machine she was, and it worked. We won 6–3 to move on to the Scotties championship game. This was a dream come true for us. Now we just had to rest and wait to see who would win the semifinals. Connie dropped into the semi after losing to us. Cathy King had advanced to the semifinals by whipping Saskatchewan's Cindy Street 12–4, so Connie played the defending champion, Cathy King, in that game. The semifinals was a surprisingly lopsided affair. Cathy won easily with a score of 10–4, and now we knew who we would play in the finals. It's pretty ironic that Cathy, Connie, and I had started together at those 1976 Canadian Juniors in Thunder Bay; and here we were together again on curling's biggest stage.

There was a packed crowd, and because we were so close to home it included a lot of people we knew. But we could not underestimate Cathy's team. They had won the Scotties the year before and had improved overall since then. Even so, we had a lot of confidence in each other and really believed we could win. Nancy had started a chant for our team that we did together before every game. We would say, "Who do you choose?" In other words, who would you choose if you had the pick of any player from any other team? The answer was, "We choose us." We all shared a feeling that year—we knew we were a special unit, even though we'd had many years of losing. We had definitely paid our dues and had learned a lot. While Cathy's team had been building over the year as the reigning Canadian champion, our team had been building for many years. That experience was invaluable. Learning to win by losing is tough, but there are so many important lessons in that process. We were still considered the underdog and some people may have looked at these teams as David versus Goliath—and at me in particular as a scrappy player who kept coming back almost every year without advancing to the play-offs. But it only mattered that we hadn't written ourselves off.

At the time, CBC was on strike, so TSN was covering the finals for the first time. Between ends, during the commercial break, music blared through the building. It was a "really rocking atmosphere," as Nancy put it. By this point, the energy of our team had synced up. It felt like magic. We'd spent so much time together and felt each other's rhythm. We sensed each other's energy and were feeding off it. And since the event was in Prince Edward Island, we were feeding off the energy of the crowd, too. And our family and friends had all made the trip over, so that added to the whole experience. That's not to say we weren't nervous, though. As in the zone as we were, there is always some anxiety before a big game. Mary-Anne remembers how incredibly nerve-wracking it was the day before the game, but on the actual day it was even worse. Her mouth was so dry she could barely swallow. Sometimes the waiting is the worst part. We all just wanted to get out on the ice and make some shots to get rid of that nervousness. There's nothing like taking that first practice slide to confirm, *Right, I know how to do this.* And those nerves always leave once the game begins.

It was a really tight game and we led 2–1 after five ends. In the sixth, we grabbed the first deuce of the game and followed it with an all-important steal in the seventh end. This really gave us full control of the game at 5–1. But we never do anything the easy way. Cathy came back with three points in the eighth end to pull to within one. Our goal was to blank the ninth end to keep last-rock advantage for the final end, which we did. So in the tenth end, with a one-point lead, I remember the nerves, the energy, and trying to stay calm. With my last rock, I faced two Team Canada rocks in the four-foot. I needed to hit the top one and roll far enough to get a full piece of the button.

Nancy was holding the broom, and I slid down to the other end to get set up, my heart racing. As I made my way down the ice, there was a roar from the crowd. I tried to lower my heart rate with deep breaths. It had been seventeen years since my first Canadian win, and there had been years when I thought this opportunity would never happen again. But here it was. I stepped into the hack, and the arena went so quiet. It was like everyone was holding their breath for me. I slid out, released the rock, and knew it was perfect right out of my hand. I remember Mary-Anne saying afterwards that she was concentrating on not "burning" it. If a player from the same team accidentally hits a rock while sweeping, it is removed from play, so she was trying to keep herself from shaking and hitting the stone with her broom. And Kim was at the back of the house, trying to keep her wits about her because she was judging the line. I hit the top stone flush on and rolled just far enough to be in the full four-foot to count as the winning point.

I fell to the ice and kissed it. It was a feeling like no other: pure euphoria. It felt different from the first time I'd won the Nationals. There had been so many years of losing since the win in 1982. All of the dedication and work since that time, and never giving up—it was an experience beyond words. It was the perfect script for our team to win. Not only had it been seventeen years since I last won, but we were playing so close to home with family members there. And everyone except Mary-Anne was in their late thirties. We were not exactly spring chickens. In my entire career, this would be the win I would cherish the most. And it was such a treat to win with those three girls. We had been through so much together, each other's highs and lows, good times and bad. We used to joke that every practice was like a therapy session. We laughed together, cried together, and now we had won together, and it was such a dream come true. I remember saying to the girls, "I don't care if I ever win another game." But it was only a joke in the moment. I really didn't mean it.

In that time between winning the Nationals, I had been married for thirteen years and had two children, and my career at the CBC was well under way. So my reaction seventeen years later was different because it had felt like I might never win again. I had never given up on the dream, but I'd felt like I could never have it all, that lightning wasn't going to strike twice. I'd had a good curling career, been to the Scotties many times, and won it once, and maybe that was all the curling gods were going to allow me. But in 1999, things came together again. And we were thankful for that. To win a championship takes a lot of skill, but also a little Lady Luck along the way, and that makes all the difference. It's funny how it seems that all of the breaks go to the victor; things bounce the right way and roll just perfectly.

We celebrated with our alternate, Laine Peters, and coach, Peter Corkum, and then ran to the sideboards for huge hugs from our families. Laine was with us for years as our alternate and went on to win the Scotties with Heather Nedohin in 2012 after she moved to Alberta. But for these Scotties, she had joined the team only four weeks prior to the Nationals. Peter, meanwhile, had been a rock for us for several years and no one believed in us more than he did. I was so happy to have Zach, Luke, and Scott there. I think Scott, more than anyone, knew what this meant to me. It was such a big relief for both of us. He'd always believed there was another championship in me.

But it wasn't just *my* win. While the focus in curling is often on the skip, this win was always about the team. Each of us knew we were totally dependent on the other and needed to have each other's backs—and we did. We fully supported each other all the time. One thing I clearly remember was Mary-Anne's reaction. She let out a blood-curdling scream that came from her toes. For those who know how calm and steady she is, this is a good memory.

The celebration when we got home was wonderful. Because of the growth of curling, it was a different atmosphere than when I won back in 1982. This time, there was wall-to-wall coverage and it seemed that everyone in Nova Scotia was watching. There was a front-page story in *The Chronicle Herald*. And we enjoyed a huge party at the Mayflower Curling Club.

Earlier in the season, I had won the Canadian Mixed Curling Championship, playing third for Paul Flemming, so I made history by becoming the first player to win two national titles in the same year. I had won the Canadian Mixed with Scott in 1993, but winning the mixed and women's championships in the same year was pretty cool. Kim went on to take my place on the mixed team a few years later, and then she won both titles in the same year also. Except she made it look easy.

THERE WERE ONLY three weeks between the Scotties and the World Championships, which were being played in Saint John, New Brunswick, that year. At least this time there was a lot less travelling involved compared to 1982, when the Worlds were in Switzerland. And there's that luck factor again: the Scotties and the Worlds both in my neighbourhood. Although I'd played in the Worlds once before, I phoned Sandra Schmirler for some advice on how to prepare and what I needed to know. Sandra had skipped her team to three Canadian and World titles between 1993 and 1997 and to an Olympic gold medal in 1998. The CBC had hired her as my replacement for its curling coverage, and she was terrific about giving me advice. Mostly, she told me to believe totally in myself, which was something I think I always needed to hear.

Sandra carried a lot of stress from her curling, because even though it's a team sport, she knew how much hinged on how she played. Certainly, Sandra's team was one we emulated in terms of playing style and the way they were so good to each other on the ice. There was never a negative word spoken. I watched all of their games from the Canadian and World championships, shot by shot, end by end, and took copious notes; if her team had one noticeable trait, it was that they knew when to play aggressively and when to play conservatively. Sandra, in particular, was really good at that. If she had a choice between a draw to the four-foot or an open hit on an opposing rock in the eight-foot, she hit almost every time. Those were the kinds of things I studied and took note of to understand what had made her team so successful. To have done what her team did, winning three World Championships and an Olympic gold medal—I didn't feel we were at that level. That was a really special team. I was always impressed with their consistency and their ability to jump all over an opponent for the littlest mistake.

I would be wearing the Team Canada uniform again, but it would be the first time for Nancy, Kim, and Mary-Anne. When our outfits arrived, we stared at those jerseys for a long time, in particular at the word *Canada*. But the elation of winning the Nationals and playing for our country was about to fade quickly. A lot of things happened to make us think it was not going to be our week to succeed—not even close. For starters, our driver was late in picking us up from the hotel for our first game and we had to hail a taxi to get us to the rink. We showed up late and didn't have much time to practice. And we were surprised by the ice conditions. They were actually tougher than when I'd played in Geneva in 1982.

Despite the ice, we started off the round robin with a pair of wins. The next day, which was Kim's birthday, we lost to Japan, the first time for a Canadian team. In that game, we came very close to running out of time. Time clocks were still fairly new in curling, brought in to speed up slow play. In the tenth end, the crowd started yelling, "Look at your time!" At first, I wasn't sure what they were saying, but when I turned and looked at the clock, panic set in. We had just over two minutes left and six of our rocks still to throw in end. We made a lot of rushed decisions and hurried throws down the stretch. The penalty for running out of time is that you lose the game. We still wound up losing the game, but not because of the clock.

Next, we played Norway's Dordi Nordby. Kim missed a shot in that game, sailing a draw through the rings. When she repeated the mistake on her next shot, Dordi laughed out loud and made a gesture to the crowd, and the crowd laughed. After the game, with Kim standing near enough to hear, Dordi told the media, "That's the worst Canadian team I've ever seen." Kim laughs about it now, and is good friends with Dordi, but at the time she wanted to clock her with her broom.

It was difficult heading into our final game, since we knew our 3–5 record wasn't good enough to get us into the playoffs. But the game was still important. The Canadian Curling Association had told me that if we didn't win this last game, Canada would face relegation, meaning our country wouldn't be guaranteed an automatic spot in next year's Worlds. I left a note for Kim and Nancy, who had gone out that night for a couple of drinks, explaining the situation. They arrived at the game ready to play. Even though we had not done well overall, we were still proud to be Canada's team and none of us wanted to go home with the added shame of losing Canada's guaranteed spot for the next year.

We arrived at the game determined to beat Denmark. We played really well for the first five ends, but at the end of the fifth Kim felt an awful pain in her back after throwing a rock. She suddenly couldn't move and needed to be wheeled to the dressing room. I didn't think it would be fair to bring Laine, our alternate, in at the midway point in such a crucial game. Laine has tons of talent, but we decided that it would best to continue with three players. But there was a downside: With just three of us, we had only one sweeper instead of two, and everything felt like a scramble. It was a crazy game, but we managed to win 9–5, preventing relegation.

Dad and his girls when the family was small. I'm in the terrible twos phase on Dad's lap, Sheila is the blondie on the left, followed by Roseanne, Barb, and Maureen.

Christmas 1979. In the foreground are Stephen, Mom, and Stephanie. In the back (from the left) are Barb, Sheila, Monica, me, Roseanne, Maureen, Dad, and Jennifer. The photo was done on a ladder with a self-timer long before the selfie stick was invented.

With my beautiful mom.

In 1984, just before Scott and I got hitched.

With Scott, Zach (left), and Luke (right), the evening of Dad's funeral, when we celebrated his life in a way he would have enjoyed, with the Malachi Polar Bear Swim. The skies cleared and the water at Hubbards Beach calmed just as we started the swim!

Celebrating our Canadian Mixed win in 1993 with Tom Fetterley and Helen Radford.

In 1982, before the big win. That's me on the left, then Kay Zinck, Monica, and Barb. (courtesy Curling Canada)

Being interviewed by CBC's Don Wittman following our win in Regina at the very first Scotties in 1982. Later, it was autographed by my two heroes, Don Wittman and Don Duguid, for encouragement.

It's a fuzzy picture, just like the 1982 World Championships in Geneva were for us. We finished out of the playoffs round, which was dismal for Canada. The big glass windows in the background caused a lot of ice headaches when the sun shone in.

Former World and Brier champion Pat Ryan started these curling cards. Do you think they are as valuable as an old Gretzky hockey card?

At the 1992 Olympics with Don Duguid. It was a beautiful setting and town, but the ice conditions were horrific for the curlers.

On-the-job bungee jumping at the Commonwealth Games in New Zealand. And they thought I screamed loudly when I curled. Did I say I'd do anything for my job?

Kim and Mary-Anne sweeping hard at the 2001 Scotties. (Andrew Klaver Photography)

Many people told me I had Maurice Richard's eyes when I curled. I took that as the ultimate compliment. (Andrew Klaver Photography)

A common scene: strategy talk, with me, Nancy, and Kim gabbing, and Mary-Anne waiting until we were done to give us the solution. (Andrew Klaver Photography)

Waiting for the measurement in the 2001 extra-end Scotties final. We won by a millimetre. I was in shock. (Andrew Klaver Photography)

Kissing the trophy after the extra-end measurement win in 2001. Winning is so sweet. (Andrew Klaver Photography)

Swan song. At the 2013 Scotties I played second for Mary-Anne. It was so sweet to be back and say good-bye. Jenn Baxter is on the left, then Kim, Mary-Anne, and me. Great memories. (Andrew Klaver Photography and Curling Canada)

Fortunately, Kim's back problem healed in a couple days, but our experience in the Worlds had been, in a word, sad.

We had been excited to play in the Worlds and it was so close to home. The crowd was rooting for us and the energy was electric. But everything we did seemed to turn out wrong. It was frustrating and depressing. The whole experience felt like a bad dream. It was an emotional roller-coaster: We had been at the top three weeks earlier and after the Worlds we were lower than low. Mostly, it was embarrassing. It was also one of those instances where the harder we tried, the worse things got.

Back home, we had to do an online chat at one point in which people were allowed to ask us whatever they wanted. As you can imagine, it wasn't fun. Many Canadian curling fans thought that because we played so poorly in the Worlds, it must have been a fluke that we won the Scotties. It was harsh criticism and we were fragile enough to think that maybe they were right. It takes a thick skin to deal with such a disappointing loss and go back to the drawing board. The criticisms, while warranted, really hurt. Curling fans might have been upset that we didn't make the playoffs, but no one was more upset by it than I was.

Regardless of what had happened, I did not have time to dwell on it. Curling doesn't bring in enough money to make a full-time living from it. In fact, we use all our vacation time to play in cashspiels and the other tournaments. So I immediately went back to working for the CBC and jumped right back into being a mom. Getting back to everyday life would always bring me back to normal— especially Mommy mode, because the kids didn't care if I won or lost. The CBC had been nothing but supportive too, giving me the time off that I needed. I was always grateful to them, and getting back to work was good for me. It was always a kind of therapy for me to move on to something else.

THE NEXT YEAR, in 2000, we returned to the Scott Tournament of Hearts in Prince George, British Columbia, this time as Team Canada. As mentioned, because we'd won the previous year, we were automatically in the tournament without having to go through the provincial qualifying process. It can be an advantage or disadvantage, depending on your team's preparation and mentality. Some teams prefer to go through the routine of having to qualify for the Nationals, because it provides competition and confidence to prepare for the next level. We weren't used to not having to go through the provincial qualifying process, and I think we really missed that. We didn't know how to put ourselves in the pressure situation we needed to get ready for the Nationals.

That whole season, we were loosey-goosey, playing cashspiels and smaller tournaments. When we got to the Scotties, we were totally unprepared for the stress of the games. We still had "imposter syndrome" (a great term supplied by Nancy) after the 1999 season because of our horrible experience at the Worlds. We decided that Nancy would help me call strategy, because she was the brain trust of the team. So, instead of having Kim with me calling shots in the house, Nancy acted as vice-skip and kept throwing lead rocks. It worked out perfectly. She and I had the same instincts when it came to style of play. Normally, the vice-skip (or mate, as we refer to the position in Nova Scotia) is behind the house with the skip, but Kim really didn't want anything to do with that. She just wanted to sweep her guts out and make her shots. Not that she isn't good at strategy—she is—but she preferred to use her energy in other ways. It was the right fit for our team.

At the 2000 Scotties, we won our opening game, beating New Brunswick 11–6. It felt good to be off to a strong start, but then we lost 7–2 to Manitoba's Connie Laliberte in the second game. A game I'll always remember from that tournament was the one against Kay Zinck, my former teammate from the 1982 Canadian title (she was Kay Smith back then), who skipped the Nova Scotia team. We lost 10–8, and things just started going south from there. We finished with a 5–6 record and didn't qualify for the playoffs. But we knew right away the mistakes we had made in terms of preparation. We hadn't found a way to put ourselves in stressful situations throughout the season, like we were used to during the Provincials.

While we were feeling sorry for ourselves at the closing banquet, TSN announcer Vic Rauter read a message from Sandra Schmirler to all of us. We all knew Sandra was battling cancer and her condition was getting worse. She was supposed to be in Prince George working for CBC, but things had deteriorated quickly and she was moved to palliative care. This came as such a shock. Vic read her message and the entire room went silent. Her note was about keeping perspective: "There are other things in life besides curling, which I have found." It was such a profound message for our team, because we were moping about losing. Sandra passed away a few days later at age thirty-six and it was just the saddest thing. The entire country mourned her loss. She had made such a huge connection with people. Curling fans everywhere loved her and her cancer story riveted the nation. She was the quintessential girl next door who had dominated the game. I flew to Regina for her funeral, which was broadcast live by CBC. Her death had such an impact on our team, because her team had been such a role model for ours. She is still missed.

AFTER OUR DISMAL showing as Team Canada in the 2000 Scotties, we were back to the old drawing board. We would have to go through the provincial playdowns to get back to the Scotties, so we approached the following season differently. We knew we had to get a lot better, but as mothers and career women we couldn't afford the time away from home to do all of the western bonspiels. There really are no professional curlers. Everyone who competes at the highest level also has a professional career or some sort of regular job. So instead, we convinced the competitive male curlers in Nova Scotia and Atlantic Canada to allow us to participate in their bonspiels as a way of helping us improve competitively. The men were terrific and it made such a big difference to our game. Every time we played a men's team, we wanted to make a decent game of it. We couldn't afford to miss shots or we'd get crushed. We learned something from every game, and it proved to be very beneficial. We played teams skipped by Mark Dacey, Paul Flemming, Shawn Adams, and Brad Gushue, but because of the way the draws unfolded we never played against my husband, Scott. The experience of playing men's teams allowed our team to compete at a high level without having to leave the province. It was a win-win for us.

We were very conscious of how we could make curling work with our families and our jobs. We had certain rules, including that we never played back-to-back weekend tournaments, and we limited our travel. Some people criticized us for this, but our priority was to try to improve while still being home to make supper and help the kids with their homework. Because the four of us were all mothers, we had to figure out a way of making curling work so that our kids weren't compromised in any way. We designed our schedule around our children, practising when the kids were in school and never at night (so we could tuck them into bed), and that left us reasonably guilt free. We were all happy that we never missed out on the day-to-day stuff. It's a delicate juggling act that a lot of curlers face, and this is what worked for us.

We also made the critical move of bringing someone in to help us with mental conditioning. When a team wins the Scotties, it becomes eligible for funding by Sport Canada to cover things like personal training, physiotherapy, massages, and (most importantly for us) mental training. In 2001, we approached Ken Bagnell, president of Canadian Sport Centre Atlantic, to be our mental trainer. Ken linked high-performance athletes with mental trainers, physiotherapists, and medical people. He had no curling background, but like any sports psychologist he understood that the psyche and headspace of any athlete is crucial to his or her success. It's all about mental toughness and training—learning how to not let anything bother you. Or if something does, allowing yourself to have a sounding board to get back to normal and get your head to a positive, confident place. Canadian Curling Association rules had changed to allow certified mental trainers to play the role of coach and be allowed on the ice. It became known as the Ken Bagnell rule. To have someone like Ken on your side is gold. He had assigned a few people to work with our team as sports psychology coaches before, but we never felt a connection with them. So we asked Ken if he would step into that role himself. Lucky for us, he did.

Ken got us talking the right language, so that we would know never to criticize one another, to think about what we were saying and doing, and to make sure we prepared the right way. He made sure we understood the importance of getting enough sleep and proper nutrition. He put us on a schedule and made sure we stuck to it.

He also started organizing team meetings, and forced us to ask tough questions of ourselves. We had always done that, but in a disorganized way, so he was a good facilitator for us, prompting both questions and answers. He was particularly helpful in helping me to settle my emotions. I used to get physically ill before games. I couldn't eat. But Ken would try to be rational about it, and just kept talking me off the ledge. He would present the facts, telling us that if we executed the way we can, we'd be successful. He also made me realize that getting to a heightened level before games was part of the process that helped me play well. Getting butterflies before events is commonplace for any athlete in any sport; learning to control them is the key.

The thing he tried to help me with the most was getting enough sleep. At times, I was exhausted. I would be so anxious the night before a big game that I couldn't sleep, so by the end of an event I'd be physically drained. There was another reason I had trouble sleeping in general, though: I was starting to experience the cerebral spinal fluid leak that would eventually lead to me contracting bacterial meningitis. We thought it was simply a nasal infection or a cold, but I would constantly wake up coughing because the fluid was draining into what felt like my lungs while I slept. Of course, we didn't know what the true problem was, but I would have had sleep issues anyway because of my anxiety. I thought I needed to be great every single time I played, and that anxiety affected my teammates. Ken helped everyone on the team recognize that they didn't need to be concerned if I appeared anxious, because that was my way of preparing. He also taught me how to take a slow and steady approach so that when a critical shot was needed, I knew I was not going to miss. Ken always delivered, always got us in the right spot. We were so interdependent—a curling team always is. It wasn't just the four of us. Along with Laine (our alternate) and later Mary Sue Radford, we were a six-person squad, all helping each other out.

I can get very intense when I'm competing. A lot of people who know me as a reporter, mom, or friend might not believe that. But on the ice, a different part of me comes out. While I'm very demanding of myself, I am also generally positive, searching for a solution to help me improve. My teammates were more than used to how I get when I'm curling, but Ken found ways to ground me and make me believe in myself more. He made me understand that everything I did had implications for the team. So whatever my mood was, whether I was beating myself up, working to improve, or joking around, Ken would make sure it was constructive for everyone. Mostly he made me realize that I did need some anxiety and intensity as the fuel that helped me to win, and he encouraged me to embrace that and work with it. So, just like working with a regular psychologist, in addition to team sessions I had many individual sessions with him through the years, in which I could talk openly about my fears and they would dissipate. He had me read mental strategy books; as well, I kept a journal and meditated. After working with Ken for a while, I remained an intense person but the anxiety and negative internal chatter stopped.

When people who didn't know me would watch me on the ice, they would always comment on how intense I looked. My fun side comes out in other settings (when I get laughing,

I laugh a lot), but on the ice I am ultra-serious. In the late 1990s and early 2000s, the game was growing and changing a lot, from an amateur feel to a more professional setting. The mental conditioning I was doing is standard now. And oh, how I wish it had been around in 1982, when we were all just trying to figure it out on our own.

Using sports psychology gave us the upper hand. We were ahead of our time. Thanks in large part to Ken, we trained and conditioned like no other team. We felt it was working, but I don't think any of us expected what would come next.

CHAPTER 7
THE CHAMPIONSHIP RUN

Going into the 2000–2001 season, Ken Bagnell became increasingly crucial to our preparation. It was a new experience for him, working with a team wanting to play at a peak level in a national competition. He had been used to working with athletes more in one-on-one situations. But Ken saw our team dynamic and figured out how to manage me, in particular, to improve our play. We noticed the difference throughout that season. We were all good friends, but now we had a new system for relating to each other. And individually, we were each getting into the mindset that worked for us. After our poor showing at the 2000 Scotties, we were eager to get back there. When we won the Provincials, we knew that the 2001 Scotties would be different. It would be a totally new experience for Ken, as he hadn't worked with us in a national competition.

The Scotties took place in Sudbury, Ontario, that year. We opened with three consecutive victories, beating Ontario, Alberta, and Quebec, then lost games to New Brunswick,

Prince Edward Island, and Newfoundland/Labrador. Ken arrived on the fourth day of the tournament because work commitments had prevented him from being there earlier. He had no idea that a team's coach could go on the ice to join his squad during the fifth-end break. When we spotted Ken, we told him to join us during the break, so he jumped over the boards, which had us howling. He was wearing sneakers—it took him a year and a half to finally buy a pair of curling shoes. Ken was all smiles, too. I think he realized that he still had some learning to do as far as the protocol of coaching in a national curling competition.

We'd been playing well, but were relieved when Ken arrived. We were playing Team Canada's Kelley Law and leading 5–1 at the break, feeling pretty good. After nine ends we led 7–4, but last rock belonged to Team Canada and Kelley scored three in the tenth end to tie it. Then, in the eleventh end, Kelley stole one to win the game. To this day, Kim is still sick about what happened in that game, because she believes that she and Mary-Anne made a sweeping mistake on my final shot. But if it hasn't been made clear yet, we were a team and succeeded or failed together.

This loss became a turning point for our team. Our record after that game was 3–4 and we were in danger of not making the playoffs. It is almost impossible to make the playoffs with five losses. But we had a bigger issue: Kim wanted to quit because she was so frustrated about the loss to Kelley. This is when Ken helped us all.

Our team relationship was all about understanding and trust, so that we could be very open and confident about what needed to be said. Part of this was helping the individual members of the team to succeed. Another part had to do strictly with me as the skip. Here again, Ken knew what to do.

He laid out Kim's choices: She could quit and go home, or she could use the angst, energy, and anger and "touch the doorknob." This was an expression he used with us—do whatever you need to do in the game and then when you get back to your hotel room, touch the doorknob. That's the cue to let everything go and move on to the next game. Whatever individual emotions we were carrying because of that difficult loss, after our meeting with Ken we came together with a single focus. It would prove to be the foundation for our success. Ken pulled us out of our wallowing and gave us something else to think about—something positive. He facilitated us in discussing things individually and as a team. He had been helping us work on our mental skills, saying we couldn't just turn them on at will, so we had to practise them all the time. He worked with each of us on individual aspects, too. With me, it was helping me to understand that losses weren't always my fault just because I was the skip. That was something I struggled with, and we worked to rephrase my thoughts. He had me celebrate my ability rather than dwell on the losses. We were going to lose games, but if we won 80 percent of them that was great. I tended to focus on the one shot that got away and then my thoughts would spiral out of control into a doomsday scenario. He made me more sensible.

Ken saved our curling lives in that tournament. We got back on track, winning our next four games to finish the round robin portion with a 7–4 record. It was good enough to put us in a three-way tie for second place behind Team Canada, which had an 8–3 record. Fortune smiled on us, too. Prince Edward Island needed to lose its last game for us to avoid having to play in a tiebreaker to make the playoffs. They had a 4–0 lead over Quebec after five ends, but ended up losing 6–4 and had to play Ontario in a tiebreaker to advance. You'd think I would have been watching that game anxiously, but with the round robin over for us, I didn't even pay attention to the final games. Instead, I watched a DVD of *Gladiator*. It was one of my inspirational films, because it's the ultimate story of survival. In our minds, *we* were warriors—and we were there fighting to stay alive. The TV commentators didn't think we could win. Mind you, we'd never been the top pick to win.

Once the dust settled after the round robin, we'd placed second overall. Ken had us in the proper headspace, which he consistently did, having restored our confidence. Confidence is a very fragile thing, and it's different for everyone. When you have it, you want to bottle it and keep it forever. On most days we had the ability to make almost every shot, but we needed to have the right mental attitude with a lot of positive talk. My mind, in particular, could lapse into a "here we go again" mode, because I had been disappointed many times throughout the years. Having Ken keep us in a positive frame of mind was really important for us.

So, despite our slow start and Kim briefly wanting to quit, Ken had gotten us back on track. In the playoffs, we faced Kelley Law's team in the opening round for the one-two game. By this time, Kim had taken a page out of my playbook, so to speak, thinking we were going to win the tournament and no one was going to stop us. We all felt that way. Whatever blips we'd had up to that point, we knew how to move forward. As Kim says, we had worked and scratched and clawed to get there. In only a few days, Kim had firmly left behind the idea of quitting and felt like we couldn't lose. We had overcome our difficulties as a group.

The game was a tough one, but we came out on top. After five ends we trailed 3–2, but finished strongly to win

7–4. Kelley's team then had to play Sherry Middaugh's Ontario team in the semifinals. When Kelley beat them, it set up a rematch between us. We were going to play the defending champions in the finals.

Kelley's team was mentally strong and well coached by Elaine Dagg-Jackson. The night before the finals, there was a big reception for all past Scotties champions. Jan Betker, who had played third on Sandra Schmirler's team, was there. She came up to me, put her hands on my cheeks, and said, "Colleen, you guys are going to win this thing. Go to your destiny." She said it with such gusto. "Go to your destiny" became our new mantra. It meant a lot coming from such a great champion. I didn't tell her then that we copied every-thing Sandra's team had done.

The championship game turned into a barnburner. Kelley led 5–2 after seven ends—but that was our "lucky score." Whenever we trailed 5–2, we always seemed to rebound. And that's what happened. We scored three in the eighth end and stole one in the ninth to lead for the first time in the game. Kelley scored one in the tenth to force an extra end. Extra ends are always nerve-wracking, but there was some-thing else to be concerned about. Frost was building up on the ice from humidity in the building, and draw weight was becoming illusive. Draw weight is the term used for the delivery speed of the stone; you have to judge how hard to throw the stone so it rests where you want. Frost on the ice is a curler's worst nightmare, because it makes draw weight so heavy and so hard to determine.

So, my last rock was not the prettiest. I needed to hit and roll off an outside stone— it's known as an in-off. My stone would then have to rest closer to the button than Kelley's shot stone (counting point), sitting in the back eight-foot ring. The commentators were saying that I should shoot a draw—just get my stone to rest in the house for a tying point. Normally, that would have been the right call, but they didn't realize that because of the frost buildup, throwing a draw would have been a stab in the dark. They were surprised when I put the broom down out in the weeds. An in-off is not an easy shot, but it was the best option. I stepped into the hack, but it was slippery from all the moisture in the air. So I ran over to our broom bag and grabbed a big, green, hand-knit curling sock to put in the hack to prevent myself from slipping. I can assure you, this had never been part of my pre-shot routine. The socks had been made by Kim's aunt awhile before, and I think we'd lost the other one. But I kept the remaining sock with us all the time because I'm crazy superstitious and believed it was our lucky charm.

I stepped back into the hack and threw an out-turn hit— my bread-and-butter shot. I was shouting the entire way down the ice: "Curl, curl, curl!" Just when it looked like it wouldn't roll enough, it curled a little bit. After the hit and roll, when the rock finally stopped, no one could tell whether Kelley or I had the closest rock to the button for the winning point. The officials had to take a measurement. Kim was sure our stone was closer, but I was always bad at eyeballing that. We all stood on the sidelines watching the official measure. Actually, I couldn't watch because I was so nervous. It was the longest two minutes of our lives. When the official finally pointed to our stone as the winner, Nancy jumped up and down and I cried. We celebrated, hugged, and screamed with joy and relief. The game had been characteristic of the entire tournament for us. We'd been down for most of it, but had scrapped our way back in. And how it all unfolded, winning in an extra end on a measurement, felt like divine intervention. But when we'd had to play well, we had played really well. There were so many "must-make" throws in that tournament, and we just took them one shot at a time, with Ken always reminding us to play "moment to moment." Most people considered us lucky, because no one believed in us, but we believed in ourselves. Of course, we had help from that "magic sock." In my long list of crazy superstitions, that green sock had lots of magic in it.

After this win, I was asked by the media if I considered myself in the same class as Sandra Schmirler, Connie Laliberte, and Vera Pezer, all of whom skipped teams to three Canadian titles. I didn't think I was in their company. They were legends in my mind. There's a difference between a Wayne Gretzky or a Mario Lemieux and a grinder. When you look at somebody like Sandra Schmirler or Connie Laliberte, and now of course Jennifer Jones, you're looking at the elite. I always felt like I was a working-class kind of athlete. But we were back on top, wearing Canada on our backs once again, and we were so proud of the work we'd done to get there.

THE 2001 WORLDS took place in Lausanne, Switzerland. I suppose it would have been easy to dwell on past trips to the Worlds, but we weren't thinking about what had happened to us two years earlier in Saint John, or what I'd experienced in 1982 in Geneva. It's never a good idea to look back too far, and Ken was keeping us all in the present moment. He kept drilling into us that the past is the past and while we learn from it, we get used to putting it away. As an athlete, it is necessary to move on. We arrived in Switzerland in plenty of time to get ready, but I wasn't sleeping the first while. I was horribly jet-lagged and exhausted and had problems adjusting to the time change. As well, Kim was battling a cold and coughing.

We started off slowly, losing our first two games. Ken kept us in the right place, though, and we remained confident. He made us think one shot at a time, one end a time, one game at a time—don't look behind and don't look too far ahead. Still, this wasn't the start we wanted. Kim and I were roommates and talked that night after our second loss. We simply decided to toughen up. We made a pact between the two of us to make our shots. We're pretty sure Mary-Anne and Nancy made the same pact in their room.

Between the promises we made to ourselves and Ken's words, something changed after that evening. We rebounded to win our next seven games, and finished tied for first with Anette Norberg of Sweden. However, we were placed first overall because we had beaten her team in head-to-head play. The playoff system in the Worlds is different from that in the Scotties. There are two semifinal games—the top team overall plays the fourth-place team and the second- and third-place teams face off—and there are no second chances if you lose. We played Lene Bidstrup's team from Denmark and were down 5–2 at one point—but, again, that score had always been a lucky one for us. We went on to win 10–6 and were set to face Anette's team in the finals after she won her semifinal game.

Sweden is a perennially strong team at the Worlds and Anette's team was no exception. They would go on to become arguably the most successful team in the women's game, winning two Olympic gold medals and three World Championships. Our strategy against this powerhouse was pretty much the same as when we played any team: Don't be aggressive when we didn't have hammer (the last-rock advantage in an end), and play for the deuces (two points) when we did. We opened the game with last rock, but through the first four ends we had nothing cooking. Each of those ends was blanked as we patiently waited for a chance for a deuce. In the fifth end, we finally took a point. Sweden blanked the sixth end, and the seventh was a turning point when we stole two more points. It was a grind of a game, and another stolen point in the eighth end had us out in front 4–0. In the ninth, Anette started to turn things around, scoring two. So, going into the tenth end we were up 4–2, but that is a narrow lead, especially against such a skilled team. But with the elusive World Championships within our reach, this time we would not be denied. At the end of the game I had an open hit to score one for a 5–2 victory.

Finally, we had won the Worlds title. The first feeling that came wasn't joy, but relief. We had lost in 1999 in Saint John, and I had lost in Geneva in 1982. There's no better feeling than winning, but even after controlling that final game and playing the way we knew we could, it was still such a relief. And really, it also felt like redemption. To be able to say we were World Champions meant a lot to all of us. We walked down the ice holding hands—all six of us, including Laine and Ken—and it felt so sweet to be on top of the world. Everyone had their families there, too, so we had a large entourage with us in Switzerland and it was all so amazing.

Even with the World Championships over, there was still something for us to aim for. Winning the 2001 Nationals had given our team a berth in the 2001 Canadian Olympic Curling Trials. They were being held in December, eight months after the Worlds. Ten men's teams and ten women's teams would compete in separate divisions to qualify for a chance to represent Canada in the 2002 Winter Olympics in Salt Lake City. Curling had gone from a demonstration sport in 1988 to a full-medal sport in 1998, and obviously one of our goals was to play in the Olympics.

The Trials were held at the Regina Agridome. Curling has a huge following in Regina, and the Agridome was the setting for my first Canadian title back in 1982, a lifetime ago. The arena has a seating capacity of six thousand and was filled for all of the games. Teams qualified by winning the Canadian men's and women's championships in the previous four years, or based on their number of top-three finishes if they had not placed first. We knew we'd be up against the best teams Canada had, and we really prepared for the Olympic Trials. As reigning World Champions, we felt confident and ready, but the Trials are a beast to win. It seems as if everyone in it is so strong; if you want to understand the depth and strength of curling in Canada, go to an Olympic Trials. Any team there can win it.

The women's field was stacked. It included former Canadian champions Kelley Law and Cathy King; three squads from Saskatchewan skipped by Sherry Anderson, Amber Holland, and Michelle Ridgway; and the always-strong rink from Ontario skipped by Saskatchewan native Sherry Middaugh. We opened with a win over Michelle Ridgway, then lost to Sherry Anderson, but rebounded with wins over Amber Holland and Cathy King. We followed that with a loss to Heather Fowlie from Alberta and a win over Sherry Middaugh. We were 4–2 with three games to go, which was a pretty good place to be in the standings. We were in the thick of the race. We lost a tight game to Kelley Law, but finished with wins over Sherry Fraser of British Columbia and Marie-France Larouche of Quebec. We ended the round robin with a 6–3 record—good enough to tie Sherry Anderson for second place (Kelley Law's team finished first).

We'd achieved our first goal: make the playoffs. Now we had a crack at being the Canadian Olympic team. We were just two wins away. Our opponent in the semifinals was Saskatchewan's Sherry Anderson, the crowd's favourite.

The game turned in Sherry's favour very early in the first half, when she made a difficult shot through a narrow opening to score three and go up 5–2. While being down by three is something we usually didn't panic over—and after all, this was our lucky score to be down by—this time we had trouble mounting a comeback. The Anderson rink was on fire. We lost 9–5, and just like that our Olympic run was over. Sherry went on to play Kelley Law in the finals and lost 7–3. But at that point, it didn't matter much to us.

We were disappointed, but we had played a strong tournament at the level we knew we could. We didn't blow any shots or make any bad calls; we simply got beat. We were still proud of what we'd accomplished that year, and began focusing on the next Canadian championship. I still had dreams of playing in the Olympics, but since we wouldn't get another crack at it for four years, it was time to get back to work.

THE 2002 SCOTTIES took place in Brandon, Manitoba. We returned as Team Canada, and after the experiences of winning at Worlds and competing at the Olympic Trials, we were really prepared. But we took nothing for granted. We had mapped out every day until the end of the season, committing ourselves to a strict practice schedule and playing in cashspiels for extra competition experience. To reinforce the drive we all felt, Ken drew up a contract that showed our commitment, so we could look each other in the eye and know we'd all "signed on the dotted line" and nothing would get in the way (barring family emergencies, of course). This wasn't a metaphor; we had a real contract. Ken put together a few clauses on respecting one another as teammates. We had spent so much time together, and we were like sisters who sometimes scrapped even though we loved each other. So this contract was really about defining our relationships with some parameters.

Most teams get to a point in the Scotties when they hit a wall, because of either the pressure involved or some other factor, and their performances start to sag. Because we stuck to some pretty strict rules, our performance actually improved. We always had one night when we would get together with our families—usually on Tuesdays—but otherwise it was all about sleeping, restoring, and renewing. I had a hard time eating due to pre-game nerves, so I would have to make a point of getting some food in me right after a night game. It was something I had battled throughout my career. Ken continued to help me, too. He always positioned himself so that we could talk at any point in a game to get me back on track. At the end of every end, I would touch base with Ken and then reconnect with the team about our plan for the next end.

We opened the 2002 Scotties with a 7–5 loss to British Columbia, but scored a 10–4 win over Prince Edward Island in our next game. It wasn't the best start, but we were feeling confident and playing well. Next, we were up against two giants: Jennifer Jones's Manitoba team and Cathy King's Alberta team. We could see that Jennifer would become a giant in the women's game. She hadn't yet won her five Canadian women's titles and her Worlds and Olympics crowns, but her skill and determination were obvious at those 2002 Nationals. Still, we won both games, and afterwards it was smooth sailing in the round robin for the most part. We finished with an 8–3 record, tying with Manitoba and Ontario for second place, one win behind Sherry Anderson's first-place Saskatchewan team. We had beaten both Manitoba and Ontario in the round robin, so we were awarded second place overall.

We were playoff bound again, facing Sherry Anderson in the battle of the one-two teams. Sherry won that game 6–3, advancing to the finals. As the loser of that game, we moved on to the semifinals to play Sherry Middaugh's Ontario team, which had won the third- and fourth-place game. We had beaten them 8–5 in the round robin, so we felt good going into that game. We stuck with our strategy and repeated the win, this time 8–6 in a really exciting game. Once again—and for the second year in a row—we were in the finals, this time facing Sherry Anderson's team.

Sherry had defeated us twice so far in the tournament and twice before that in the 2001 Olympic Trials. It was hard not to think that she had our number. After losing to Sherry in the opening round of the playoffs, we'd had a team meeting to ask ourselves if we had the competitive desire to win the finals. We simply did not want to lose our winning feeling. We had responded well, winning the semi-finals, so perhaps it was right that we were facing Sherry again. I was peaceful heading into the finals, and that came about through Ken's efforts. I met with him in the morning before the game. Mental toughness and mental peace is hard work, and back then I worked at it constantly. I read numerous books on the topic and tried to bring that tough-ness into every facet of my life, whether it was work (such as not getting flustered at deadline time), or being in the moment with my kids, or just being positive. To everyone else, it seemed like nothing could bother me, and I think that feeling helped gel the team. Ken knew that if he could keep me focused, the rest of the team would benefit too.

After five ends against Sherry, we were leading 3–2. It was still either team's game to win, and there was a lot of anticipation in the air. You could feel the crowd waiting for something to happen. In the sixth end, we really broke it open, stealing three when Sherry missed an attempt to remove two of our stones with a tricky double takeout. After that, we kept playing our game and protected our lead. We won 8–5. According to the game statistician, I played the best game of my career, shooting 99 percent (I wonder what happened to that last percent?), but we all played really well in that game. The end result was what we had been trying to accomplish all year—be an all-around great team, consistent and mentally tough. Playing a high-level game means doing the mental work needed to be strong and not get distracted. And we also had that magic ingredient: team chemistry.

It is really hard to win back-to-back titles in Canada, because there are so many great teams. Winning that game meant a lot in and of itself. But we'd also broken a record: I became the first skip to win four Canadian national titles. I was asked by the media about the magnitude of it; their questions were similar to the ones I got in 2001 when I had tied the record. I still thought that Sandra's team was the greatest in the world. I still thought of myself as a grinder.

The media asked Sherry about her team's experience, too. She was disappointed after leading throughout the tournament, and found it difficult to put into words. But she found some great ones. She said it was a bad end to a good week and that there were probably three hundred teams that would have loved to have played in the finals. She summed things up by saying it hadn't been their goal to get to the finals and lose. That was a tough year for her squad, as they'd also lost the Olympic Trials finals.

I had been through similar experiences in 1980 and 1984, and knew exactly how Sherry felt. No matter how well you play in a tournament of this magnitude, if you lose in the finals it stays with you for a long time. Some skips never even get a second chance because, again, there are so many great teams in Canada.

THROUGHOUT THE SEASON we had joked that if we repeated as Canadian champions, we'd have to play the Worlds in Bismarck, North Dakota. We wanted to win the Nationals, of course, but for some reason we all had a negative attitude about going to North Dakota. I suppose it was simply because we had been lucky enough to be in charming Switzerland the year before, surrounded by the Alps and delicious chocolate.

It was a tough tournament and all of the teams seemed to be evenly matched. As the reigning World Champs, we felt confident going in, but something started to slip and slide once we got on the ice. We finished in a three-way tie with Switzerland and Denmark for fourth place after the round robin, all of us with a 5–4 record. We ended up playing Switzerland in one of the tiebreakers and survived that game to advance to the playoffs, where we faced Scotland's Jackie Lockhart. We had played Jackie a few times before, and felt good going into the game. Scotland is always tough, though. They are confident and love a good fight. Jackie was one of those players who when she was hot, she was really hot— and she was on fire in that semifinals, beating us 5–4.

And just like that, we were out after just one playoff game. Scotland went on to win the Worlds that year. We didn't go to the rink to watch the finals. Instead, we decided to stay at the hotel pool with our families. Imagine our surprise when Jackie's team, fresh from winning the Worlds, came into the pool area and jumped into the water with their clothes still on. We had stunned looks on our faces as we watched them celebrate. And we were maybe just a tad upset that we had lost. I don't have any excuses for what happened. There was a feeling that we weren't as hungry and motivated as we should have been. That whole tournament was pretty much a blur.

We loved being Team Canada and didn't want it to end. That summer we met several times to plan the next season, and also to try to learn from our loss in North Dakota. Overall, we liked what we were doing and had gotten into a real groove together. We were anxious to go back to the Nationals in 2003 and try to win it three times in a row.

The 2003 Scotties were held in Kitchener, Ontario, and we were feeling pretty good. Only one other skip—Vera Pezer of Saskatchewan—had won three consecutive Canadian women's titles, but none of us were thinking about history. Nancy always referred to us as a team that had just fallen off the turnip truck, and in some ways that's all we were. We were not bumblers (we were very well organized and worked really hard at our game), but we still had that feeling of "aw, shucks, isn't this great?" And Ken had us focused on playing our game and not worrying about our opponents, the record, or anything else.

In our opening game, we played Prince Edward Island's Suzanne Gaudet, who'd skipped her Summerside foursome to championships in the 2001 and 2002 Canadian Junior tournaments and won the World Juniors in 2001. She was playing at the women's level for the first time, and came into the tournament amid much fanfare and media attention as a new, young talent poised to show her skill set against established veterans. I felt comfortable playing her because I knew what she was like as a thrower. We had already played against her several times at different events around the Maritimes. Knowing and understanding your opponent helps a lot. Even so, it was a close game. It went to an extra end, but we managed to beat Suzanne's team 8–7. Not one to prove the media wrong, Suzanne didn't lose another game, finishing first overall with a 10–1 record. We placed second with an 8–3 mark, so we were up against Suzanne's team in the opening round of the playoffs. Her team was certainly on a roll and must have been feeling confident. But so were we. We won 6–3, which qualified us for the finals for the third consecutive year.

After their amazing run, Suzanne's team wound up losing 6–5 in the semifinals against Cathy Cunningham's squad from Newfoundland and Labrador. Like Suzanne's team, we had faced Cathy's team numerous times in cashspiels; as well, she had beaten us 6–5 during the round robin. We started off going gangbusters, scoring five points in the first three ends to go up 5–0. For us, though, this was not a comfortable position, because with a 5–0 lead we needed to play defensively. We were known as a defensive team, so you would think we would have loved this situation. But we were actually more comfortable playing in tight games, or even being down a few points. Sure enough, Cathy's team rallied, picking up two points in the fourth end and stealing two in the fifth. We scored one in the six, giving us just a two-point lead, when we'd been up by five. Cathy soon erased that deficit by scoring two in the seventh, tying the game at 6–6.

This was turning into a real grind of a game. We added one in the eighth, but Cathy blanked the ninth and tied the game again with one in the tenth. Her team actually could have won it in the tenth end, but fortunately for us, a costly roll out by third Peg Goss got us out of that jam. Like other big games we'd played, this one was going to be decided in an extra end. With her final stone, Cathy attempted to draw around another stone, but she ticked the guard and her shooter rolled open. That left the door open for my favourite shot: the out-turn hit. I hit her stone and my shooter stayed in the house to count two, giving us a 9–7 win. It was our third consecutive Canadian championship, tying the record Vera Pezer had set in 1971 to 1973.

I was asked by someone in the media if I considered our team a dynasty because we had won four national titles in five years. I remember saying I wasn't ready for that. Basically, I didn't want the label. When we began as a team, I never thought we would emerge to become what we had. We'd grown so much and come so far! I was overwhelmed.

Looking back on it now, I can say we had good luck and caught a few breaks, but you make your breaks too. Ken had us developing a unified feeling, and going out and really applying it on the ice. Some teams have a look of greatness and confidence the moment they step onto the ice. I remember feeling that way about Marilyn Bodogh, who won the Scotties and Worlds in 1986, and then duplicated that ten years later with a totally new team. Similarly, I definitely was always in awe of Sandra Schmirler's team and Connie Laliberte's squad. Now, clearly, Jennifer Jones's great Manitoba rink is in a class of their own when it comes to looking like they are going to win from the moment they step on the ice. Maybe we had a little of that too.

People were waiting for us when we arrived at the Halifax airport. Our premier at the time, John Hamm, remarked: "Our

Team Canada members, representing Nova Scotia, are a great example of how combining teamwork and sportsmanship bring positive results." It was high praise, and it felt great to have our team recognized like that. We were still so proud to play for Nova Scotia. Plus, we were heading to the Worlds with renewed purpose after losing in the semifinals the year before.

THIS TIME, we were pumped for the Worlds because it was taking place in Winnipeg, a city with a crazy-strong curling base and tremendous support from fans. I had actually never played in Winnipeg before, and for me it was going to be like playing hockey in the Montreal Forum. We enjoyed the energy of the crowd right from the opening game and played really well. It was amazing. We went undefeated in the round robin with a 9–0 record, then made it ten wins in a row after beating Dordi Nordby of Norway 8–7 in an extra end in the semifinals. We were still feeling cautious, though. There was always the possibility we might not win in the finals because we understood that there's such parity in both the men's and women's Worlds. Any team could take it. Debbie McCormick of the United States beat Sweden's Anette Norberg 5–4 in the other semifinals, so it was going to be a Canada vs. USA finals for the first time at the women's Worlds.

It was such an incredible feeling playing the finals in a packed arena. We'd beaten Debbie's team in the round robin, so we thought we knew her game plan. What we didn't know was that her coach, Ed Lukowich, a two-time Canadian men's champion and one-time Worlds champion from Alberta, had changed things up. During the round robin, Debbie's team had been super aggressive, calling centre guards when they didn't have last rock and corner guards when they had hammer. There were rocks everywhere. That strategy was getting them into a lot of trouble, which is why Lukowich changed it up. The team we met in the finals was totally defensive.

When a rock was thrown out in front of the house, our style was always to play aggressively and try to draw around it to the top of the eight-foot. Our mantra, coined by Mary-Anne, was "If you call, we'll answer." Because of the rules, you can't remove any of the first four stones if they are outside the house—that's the free guard zone—but Debbie's team was throwing everything into the house. Plus, it seemed that every time we got something going in an end, they would make an incredible shot. By the time I figured out what was happening, it was the fifth-end break and they were leading 3–2 with last rock going into the sixth. They blanked the sixth end and scored one in the seventh. We blanked the eighth end and took one in the ninth. But our flow was gone. They added one more in the tenth to win 5–3. I wish I could have played smarter in that game and realized sooner that we needed to play better offence in that game. Of any loss we experienced in any of the World Championships we competed in, that one was the most disappointing.

AS ALWAYS, we did our best to look ahead. No team had ever won four consecutive Canadian men's or women's championships, but at the start of the 2004 season we weren't thinking at all about history. In my mind, winning the Canadian title the year before didn't earn us anything for the current season. Every year, I worried that we would become a bit blasé about continuing to win, and lose our hunger and drive to be the best. We needed to stay humble. Kim calls me "The Queen of Humble and Hungry." She laughs now in retrospect, but at the time she must have wondered why

I couldn't let us all off the hook for just one week. But we had to get better. In our first team meeting after the loss at the Worlds, I talked about what had happened in Winnipeg. We all knew how good we could be, but to get better we needed to focus on taking it to another level.

All of us were hungry. We wanted to keep being Team Canada, and we liked the benefits that came with it. The first time we got a free pass to the Scotties, it had hurt us because we missed out on valuable competition time. But that was no longer an issue for us. Having to qualify for the Scotties by playing in curling clubs is not easy, because the quality of the ice is not as good as in national and international tournaments. You always want to play in the best conditions, and that's on arena ice. It makes it much easier to plan strategy and make great shots when the ice is consistent. We knew that to defend our Canadian title we needed to keep working on consistent throws and mental toughness.

There were many good teams across Canada that season, yet we were so confident going into the Scotties that we didn't think there was a team that could beat us. Kim says we had an addiction to winning, and she's right. I was pretty crazy when it came to intensity and Kim was nearly the same. She hates to lose as much as I do, and that's a good combination to have in the back end of a team.

In addition to using Ken as our mental coach, we also used different technical coaches to help us improve, and each one of them helped take our game to a different level. Our first coach, Peter Corkum, of course did a lot of the ground work. We also had Scott Taylor, who went on to coach World champion Glenn Howard's rinks, come down from Ontario and work with us. Former World champion Rick Folk also spent a season with us and that was a great fit, although the distance between British Columbia and Nova Scotia was too much. We also got to work at the World Championships with Elaine Dagg-Jackson and benefitted from her insights. But the most influential person was the guy we called our guru and that was Curling Canada's high performance director, Gerry Peckham. He understood our team completely. He didn't try to change us to be something we weren't; he just kept pushing us to get a little bit better. He is based in Ottawa, but travelled to Halifax enough to help us manage our tendencies and fix any glaring issues that were popping up in our deliveries. I also spent hours on the phone with him discussing ideas and strategies. We owe him an enormous amount for always seeing our potential and encouraging us to meet that potential. He is a gifted coach.

Anyhow, back to the Scotties. The 2004 tournament took place in Red Deer, Alberta, and we may have had our greatest overall performance in that tournament. There was a lineup change for us at this event. Laine Peters, who had been our long time fifth player, had won the Nova Scotia title with her team skipped by Heather Smith. So, Mary Sue Radford joined our team as our fifth player and she was a valuable addition for us. She's an excellent sounding board and a good strategist; she helped along with Ken to keep us on track. We started off with three consecutive wins, before losing 6–5 to Heather's team. Heather was the skip but Meredith Doyle threw last stones, just like the Randy Ferbey and David Nedohin team that won four Canadian championships (plus three Worlds titles) in five years. Meredith and Heather were a very strong team, so solid, both having won Canadian Juniors titles. On the front end, not only did they have Laine Peters at second stone, but Beth Iskiw was the lead. Laine and Beth would go on to win the Scotties when they both moved out to Alberta and joined forces with

Heather Nedohin. In any event, we lost to Nova Scotia, a team that certainly wasn't intimidated by us because they saw us every day at the Mayflower Curling Club back home.

We rebounded from that loss and experienced only one more defeat in the round robin, 9–8 to Manitoba. I think I go into every Canadian championship thinking, *Yup, we could lose to Manitoba. That province breeds curlers.* We ended up playing Sherry Middaugh's team from Ontario in the one-two game of the playoffs. We had played a high-scoring game against her team in the 2002 semifinals, and this one turned into a similar contest. We were trailing 7–5 at the fifth-end break and knew it was giddy-up time. After eight ends, the game was tied up. Sherry blanked the ninth end to maintain last shot in the tenth. I remember how nerve-wracking it was to watch Sherry's rock coming down the sheet. It's hard not having the last shot. All we could do was watch her final shot as she tried to come through a tough hole and hope that she missed. We called in every jinx we had, and it worked. There's a little magic to winning after all! Sherry's shot missed and we ended up winning 9–8. We were off to another finals.

Marie-France Larouche of Quebec beat Lois Fowler of Manitoba 9–4 and advanced to the semifinals against Sherry. That game went to eleven ends, but Quebec prevailed to win 7–6. Marie-France had won the 1999 Canadian Junior Curling Championships and had such a solid team. She was considered a machine during her junior career. We had beaten Marie-France's team 9–3 in the round robin game, so we felt pretty confident playing against them in the finals. Plus, at this stage of our career we were getting pretty comfortable playing in the Canadian finals. We knew the routine well.

We led 4–2 after five ends, but I was feeling a bit flustered because I had missed some shots. I walked over to Ken and said, "I forgot how to curl." He just laughed and brought me back to a good space. He always did. He reminded me of my history of always finishing a game stronger than I started; plus, he reminded me we had a two-point lead. We stole a point in the seventh end to take full control. They scored a point in the eighth end, but we really sealed things in the ninth end with a deuce. In the tenth end, we simply had to keep things clean by removing their rocks so they would have no chance for the tie. We won 7–4 and recorded our fourth consecutive title, and fifth title overall for the team, something no team in Canada had ever done in either women's or men's play. We had worked so hard during the season, and it was gratifying to celebrate being part of history.

Our win this time actually presented a unique problem for the sponsor, Scott Paper. They have a very cool prize structure. When you win the Scotties the first time, you are given a ring with a quarter-carat diamond in it. The next time you win, the diamond is replaced by a bigger sparkling diamond. After a third win, the prize is a Rolex watch. If you win a fourth time, the prize is a trip with your whole family anywhere in the world. After our 2004 win, they gave us a choice of a Ski-Doo, Sea-Doo, or all-terrain vehicle. I chose the ATV. At the time, we joked that they would probably be glad if we stopped winning because they were running out of ideas.

As was always the case after winning the Nationals, there was little time to enjoy the feeling of victory. Heading into the Worlds in Gävle, Sweden, I knew we wanted to win another one. I didn't want another Bismarck or Winnipeg. We were focused. With every year we played, Ken got better at controlling everything behind the scenes to make sure we stayed in a bubble. Ken made it simple for us: our job was to get as much sleep as possible, eat when we could, and curl.

Once again, many family members made the trip. This time, my sister Barb and my mom travelled to be with us, as well as Scott and the kids. On the day we had off from the tournament, Scott and I went out for dinner with Barb and Mom and we talked about how Sweden reminded us of Nova Scotia, with its rugged coastline and natural beauty. I felt very relaxed and in a good space. Barb thought I was "in the zone." I suppose I was. We finished the round robin tied for second with Switzerland, at 6–3. Dordi Nordby of Norway placed first overall with a 7–2 record. We beat Switzerland 8–6 in the semifinals, and moved forward to play Dordi in the finals. She had won the Worlds in 1990 and 1991 and we had faced her numerous times before. We'd also played her in the round robin, winning that game 7–5.

After five ends we led 4–2, and scored two more in the sixth to take a commanding lead. We traded single points in the next four ends, but stayed on top. This time it was Kim who had the thrill of making the decisive shot in the tenth end, a gorgeous double takeout to run the Norwegians out of rocks. With that shot, we'd won it. I still remember Kim's big leg-kick celebration. We were solid as a team in that one, shooting 83 percent overall (pretty close to where we always were when we won). And the win was so satisfying. We had employed our KISS strategy: Keep It Simple, Stupid. As we always told ourselves, just take it a shot at a time. I didn't think anyone could beat us, because we were such a good unit, the four of us together. We had each other's backs: If one person missed, the next person would make a double. We did the mental work, so if there was a blip in the game we stayed strong, and we practised hard. We deserved this. After disappointments in the Worlds in Bismark, Winnipeg, and Saint John, it was a thrill to win this one.

Our family members joined us on the ice to celebrate with the trophy, and we sang "We Are the Champions." That felt so sweet. Family was always priority number one, so to be able to celebrate with them made us all shed a few tears. My mom was so funny. Apparently she wasn't sure what was going on, so when we won and Barb started jumping up and down, she asked Barb, "Is that it?" But Mom was really happy for us and had a blast celebrating and being very social with everyone. We also had tremendous support from our fans and supporters back home, so it was nice to win for them too.

Was there a secret to our success? Yes. We knew who we were. We also really enjoyed and respected each other and loved being on the ice together. The game was constantly changing and we had to figure out how to adapt our skill set and what worked best for our team to win. It's important to keep watching, studying, and adjusting. You can't stay static in the sport. You have to be an honest critic of yourself and find ways to keep improving. If you aren't winning, figure out what you need to do to get that much better. We had become really good at recognizing our strengths and weaknesses. But the key was always team chemistry. No team wins without it.

We were pumped after winning the Worlds again, and I think it took two months after the season ended to finally hit us that we had made history by winning four consecutive Canadian titles. That's when we thought, *Wow, that's pretty darn special.* But as they say, all good things must come to an end. Our fabulous run was about to run its course.

CHAPTER 8
ALL GOOD THINGS...

After every curling season, we would take a three-week break to recharge our batteries. Only then would we begin preparing for the season ahead, spending a good chunk of the summer connected in one way or another. Whether going to the gym together, barbecuing, or doing our sports psychology work, we had a lot of time to plan as a team. Approaching the 2005 season had a different feel, though, because of the Canadian Olympic Curling Trials, which would take place in Halifax in December. This was the event we had been waiting for. We'd had so much success in the previous four years, winning four straight Nationals and the 2001 and 2004 World Championships. But we still hadn't had a shot at the Olympic rings. We had qualified for the Trials in 2001 and placed third, but now we would have another try at it. And this time the Trials were taking place at home in Halifax—we were very excited. They were still more than a year away, but when we sat down to map out our future, those December 2005 Olympic Trials had a big circle drawn around them.

All of us on this team were from the same curling club. We'd come up together, and trained and developed together as a team. This doesn't happen now. A lot of players shift around to different teams, in different provinces. It's very rare for players to come up together like we did and continue to have that kind of success. So, getting the chance to earn an Olympics spot in Halifax was the perfect script.

We changed our routine, moving away from playing in men's bonspiels. We wanted more game situations against women's teams. Our training schedule had always driven us to our peak in February for the Nationals. We still wanted to be great in February, but the event we wanted to win the most was those Olympic Trials at the end of the year.

The 2005 Scotties took place in St. John's, Newfoundland, at Mile One Stadium. We always loved playing in Atlantic Canada. It seemed that the crowd was always cheering for some team from the area to win, so it just felt comfortable. The arena and hotel were side by side, so we didn't have the drive that we normally had in other tournaments. We could walk to the arena if we wanted to, but because of my superstitions about doing everything the same way in every Nationals—always leaving the hotel in the same order, sitting in the same seats in the van, and me carrying that lucky green sock in my coat—we decided to stick to our routine. (Yes, I still carried around the magic green sock from when we won our third national championship.) We were driving only half a block, but it was still a good routine to keep. To suddenly start walking, even if on an indoor walkway, wouldn't have worked for us. Ken, who always had us follow a routine, totally supported this.

There was another unusual quirk to this tournament. We were returning to the Scotties as Team Canada, which meant that another team was representing Nova Scotia. That year, my sister Monica was playing lead for Kay Zinck on the provincial team. Monica and Kay had been two of my team-mates in 1982 when we won the Nationals (my sister Barb was the other member of the squad). We hadn't played against Monica in several years. The media played up the story about two sisters on opposing teams vying to win one title. Basically, my feeling was that I hoped her team did well, just not against our team.

We started the tournament well enough, but when it came time to face Monica and Kay in our sixth game we had only a 2–3 record. It was a must-win game for us if we were going to have any hope of winning five straight Nationals. We played well, stealing points in three consecutive ends, and won the game 8–4. I had no qualms or nostalgia about playing my little sister. Ken had done a masterful job of making sure that whatever team I played against was simply "Team X" in my head. Kay's team finished the tournament with a 5–6 record and didn't reach the playoffs.

Monica found that tournament exhausting compared to when she had played in it with me. Of course, we were a lot younger in 1982. Also, for her, this tournament did not have "the lore of the past." We had gone into the 1982 competition driven and naive, but this time around she knew that when she played Team Canada she would be up against one of the top teams. She told me later that at one point she'd looked at our team and wondered how we'd been able to keep going all those years. But Monica readily admits that there are people who need to win more and work hard at it, and I was one of those people who could stay hungry for that long. Barb used to joke that if I put half the amount of time I spent training into running a business, I could have been a millionaire.

After our game against Kay and Monica's team, we tried to take that win and turn things around. In the end, we finished the round robin in a four-way tie for fourth with a 6–5 record. We faced New Brunswick's Sandy Comeau in a tiebreaker to try to sneak into the playoffs. New Brunswick led 5–4 after eight ends, but Sandy put the game away in the ninth when she made a great shot through a narrow opening to remove our lone rock and score four. Game over.

Just like that, our run had ended. As I was making my way back to the opposite end of the ice, I collapsed to my knees and cried. It really started to sink in then. Our run was over. But something happened that I will always cherish. Cathy King, whom I had battled against many times in my career, going all the way back to juniors, was playing at the same time as us in a tiebreaker against Ontario's Jenn Hanna. When we lost, the players on both those teams stopped and applauded us. Cathy looked over at me and bowed. It was so sweet for them to take time out of their crucial game to acknowledge our run. It was a lot to take in at the time because of our loss, but to be acknowledged by our fellow competitors was a really touching, wonderful moment that choked up every member of our team. The crowd stood and applauded us, too. Ken, always the team builder, told us the applause was in recognition of the amazing things each of us had done individually, which collectively made us a great team.

When I came off the ice, Monica gave me a hug and said, "Wow, look at this." It was all so wonderful and supportive. I think I was as emotional as I've ever been. After the game, the media asked me how I felt about the end of our team's run. It was impossible to put my feelings into words, but I tried to sum them up. I said that it's never easy to lose, even more so when you know what it is you've lost—specifically, the title of the best women's team in Canada. God knows we didn't want it to ever end. It was difficult for me when I realized what the crowd was acknowledging: the end of what we had done. I was just so crushed it was over. We all were. When Sandy Comeau was asked by the media about her team's win, she said, "I slayed the dragon." She added that we had done a lot for curling and called me a great ambassador for the sport. It was kind of her to say that.

When Cathy King was interviewed by the media, she acknowledged our amazing run and also commented on how much we had done for curling. In her opinion, we'd picked up and carried on from what Sandra Schmirler had accomplished. Later, Jenn Hanna, who beat Cathy's team in their tiebreaker, told the media she almost cried when we lost because she considered me a "total legend," and became choked up just thinking about it. She had no qualms about pausing during her game against Cathy, because she felt we deserved that standing ovation. Afterwards, Jenn handed us a beautiful handwritten letter to let us know how much our team meant to her and inspired her, which was really nice. We read it later after we'd had time to process what had happened.

Joan McCusker, who threw second stones for Sandra Schmirler and later became a curling analyst for CBC, also paid us a wonderful compliment. She called our team role models for all women athletes. That meant a lot to us then, and still does. She knew more than most because of her time playing with Sandra. They had gone through many of the same experiences our team had. And she knew our success wasn't just about the skip, but about the whole team, because each member worked together as one. It wasn't about ego or selfishness. We had one single goal.

It had been hard enough to win four consecutive Scotties, so to think we could have made it five in a row—that would have been tough. In Canada, where there are many talented players, there are always new stars and teams emerging from the junior ranks or gaining experience at the women's level and building experience. Everything had been going our way, and that's what it takes to win. You can always look at anybody who wins in curling and say, "Wow, they got that right rub" or "They got that perfect roll." There's a lot of talent on winning teams, and there's a whole lot of luck. We always thought we were living a charmed life, even in some ways that we had a team of destiny. Rubs went our way. The schedule seemed to go our way. I think we always felt the curling gods were on our side during our run. But it can all change and suddenly seem as if everything is stacked against you.

For the first time in four years, we became spectators instead of participants at the playoffs. We'd become used to being in The Show—the final game—and seeing another team in it was hard to watch. Playing in the finals and being on that one sheet with thousands of people in the stands is awesome; it's just the best feeling. But we definitely wanted to see the final game, and it was a great one. Manitoba's Jennifer Jones played Ontario's Jenn Hanna. It looked like Ontario had the game in the bag as Jennifer prepared to throw her final rock. She had to throw an in-turn hit on an Ontario stone sitting just outside the rings, then roll her shooter over to remove the Ontario shot stone that was sitting buried on the button. An in-off, as the shot is known, is tough at the best of times, but with a Canadian championship on the line it's that much more difficult. Jennifer threw it perfectly, to count four! She had the ultimate circus shot to win, and executed it to perfection in what is usually described as the greatest shot ever to win a final. It was amazing, and started the years of domination by Jennifer Jones.

So, one Jones was dethroned as another was anointed queen. Jennifer had been waiting in the wings for awhile, and she had been a machine since her time in the juniors. That was her time, and she's taken the women's game to new heights.

Mary-Anne made an interesting remark after our run ended. She told the media that it could be a blessing in disguise, because now we would have less of a target on our backs. Without that distraction, we would be hungrier for the Olympic Trials. She had a point. Ken did a really good job of rallying us and making us understand that winning at December's Olympic Trials was really what we wanted. He refocused us when we really needed that. The Trials were still ten months away, and while we had slipped at these Scotties, it was time to pick ourselves back up.

BECAUSE WE HAD gone to the Olympic Trials before, come December we arrived at the tournament ready and prepared. In every tournament we played, it was always about the journey to get there. The journey meant you practised, you did the work, you competed; but you also worked extremely hard to not think about the outcome. If you check off all the boxes of work that you need to do, the results take care of themselves. Then, suddenly, the Olympic Trials had arrived and our focus changed to "let's just win this thing." That may have been a mistake, shifting our mindset to "winning" instead of just enjoying our time together on the ice and doing the work.

Even though the Trials took place in our hometown, we stayed in the players' hotel and kept to our tried-and-true routine. Staying at home would have allowed us to fall into Mommy mode too easily. We needed to keep our minds on curling. But it soon became clear our A-game wasn't with us. After five games, we had a 2–3 record. We could feel that we didn't have what it would take to win the tournament. Three losses in the round robin at the Trials is really the limit—lose more than that and it's almost impossible to make it to the playoffs. When we lost our sixth game, we knew we were done. We finished the Trials with a 3–6 record. Do I know why we didn't have what it took to succeed? The simple answer is that we didn't play well enough. Probably, we just ran out of gas as a team. In a round robin, a team can afford to lose a game or two, but it's crucial to find your happy place—that wonderful mental place where you are full of confidence and feel like you can make any shot. Winning early is often the key, as it builds team confidence and keeps those dreaded three losses at bay. Occasionally you'll see teams rally after dropping down to four losses, but generally everyone aims to stay in that leader pack to guarantee a spot in the playoffs. But we had run out of shots; we had run out of everything.

Curling is a slippery game. On the men's side at those Trials, nobody would have picked Brad Gushue of Newfoundland to win it. The favourites were Kevin Martin, Glenn Howard, Jeff Stoughton, and Randy Ferbey. But Gushue's rink carried the hot hand and won the Trials. They even went on to capture Olympic gold in Torino.

I think all teams peak for only so long, and in hindsight we were lucky enough to have our streak last for so many years. We were pushing the curling gods to try to get us to the top one more time for the ultimate show, the Olympics, and it didn't work out. We did everything we could and felt ready, but as we all know in sports, only one team can win and it sure wasn't us.

In retrospect, Ken wasn't surprised by our loss, because some teams were passing us by doing the same things we had done. It was a very uncomfortable time for us, knowing that we were holding on at that stage, hoping to reclaim some of our magic but knowing it wasn't there. Ken said it was all about confidence, and that we were fragile at that point and it showed. As we came into the Trials we felt we were ready, but in the backs of our minds it just wasn't there.

EVEN SO, after losing at the Olympic Trials again, we half heartedly decided to enter the Nova Scotia provincial play-downs the following month. We won those and were heading back to the Scotties. It wasn't quite my normal preparation for this Scotties since I was heading to Torino, Italy, to cover the Olympics for the CBC. It was a bit surreal being in Italy as a reporter instead of a curler, because going as an athlete had been our focus for the previous few years. But if there's one trait I have, it's the ability to change hats quickly. So, I flew back just before the Winter Games' closing ceremonies to join my team at the Scotties. If there was a good omen for the Scotties, it happened in the skills competition that precedes the tournament. I won it, defeating Manitoba's Jill Thurston, and received a two-year lease on a brand new Ford Explorer as my prize.

We rediscovered our stride, finishing the round robin tied for second place with Team Canada's Jennifer Jones at 8–3. Because we had beaten her team in head-to-head play, we placed second overall. But we had a weird experience toward the latter part of the round robin. We were playing against Manitoba, and after five ends Mary-Anne had a hard time catching her breath. Mary Sue Radford, our alternate, came into the game to take Mary-Anne's place and did an amazing job. It's always hard to come into the middle of a game like that, but it was also her Scotties debut and she handled herself so well. We were leading 4–3 at that point and went on to win the game 7–6, but our concern was more about Mary-Anne's health. She had to be hospitalized, where it was discovered she had suffered a really bad allergic reaction to a perfume worn by a Manitoba player. She was treated with Benadryl to help her breathe. Mary-Anne told the media that she loves perfume, but there seemed to be one ingredient in one perfume that had made her throat close up. All competitors were later told not to wear any perfume during games.

British Columbia's Kelly Scott had finished first in the round robin, so we were playing her in the opening round of the playoffs to determine which team would go directly to the finals. They beat us 6–5 and it was actually a difficult loss. It was close, and I don't mean only the score. Curling is a game of inches, and in that game we were just on the wrong side of that inch. It was a game we felt we could have, and should have, won.

After that loss, we played Team Canada's Jennifer Jones in the semifinals. The game was tied 3–3 after five ends, but Jennifer scored three in the sixth to break it wide open. We scored a point in the seventh, but were still down by so much that we had to go for broke and gamble to try to steal. It didn't work out so well. Jennifer scored four in the eighth to go ahead 10–4. There was no point in prolonging the game. Sometimes you have to realize that it's not your day, so we surrendered.

As I told the media afterwards, the pressure of having to continually make shots takes a toll. I was asked whether we planned to continue competing and I jokingly replied, "To curl or not to curl, that is the question." I added that we loved what the game had given us over the years, but at the same time we were looking forward to getting home to relax. A lot of people had written us off after the Olympic Trials, but we came back and showed our grit and finished third overall in the Nationals.

About two weeks after the Scotties, we convened at Nancy's house to discuss the future of our team. We mutually decided that we were done. We'd been on top for a very long time and had enjoyed every minute of it, but the work needed to stay on top was too much. We were breaking up and, like the song says, it was hard to do. I think for all of us, that night was a bit dream-like. We were sitting in Nancy's family room drinking wine, and we all knew our run was over. Kim came to that meeting with the intention of handing in her pink slip, because "the carrot wasn't big enough for the effort to try and stay where we wanted to stay." So she announced that she was done, and Nancy expressed the same thing.

I understood completely. Everybody had known the end was coming, that we were more or less done. We had spent a lot of time chasing the dream and accomplished more than what we ever thought we would. We had lived the dream and checked off just about everything on our curling bucket list. We'd enjoyed an incredible run and weren't going to win anything more with that team, so the natural thing to do was to break up. It was hard enough trying to be at our best every year, trying to play great all the time. We were a great curling team, but that was never enough. We had to constantly find ways to get better, too. On top of that, we'd been juggling our real lives—family and jobs. We were worn out.

We knew it was time, but it wasn't an easy choice to make. We'd spent so much time together that we were like sisters. We scrapped like sisters and loved each other, too. We had our routines and our superstitions (me more than the others on that last point), and our own quirks as a team that worked for us. But as time goes on relationships change, and we had to concede that things weren't going to be the same any more.

Ken saw it, too. We'd had something truly special. At some point, we became the intimidating team that made others nervous to play against us. Teams knew they couldn't make any mistakes against us, and we often had that advantage. Ken believes no other team will be able to duplicate what we accomplished. I don't know if he's right, but I know that we were lucky to hit on a magic formula that worked for us; that doesn't happen often.

All around, it was the right decision. Although I do believe that if we could go back to that night, we all would have handled what came next a lot differently. But that's the value of hindsight. We couldn't foresee the media storm that was coming.

Even though we agreed to break up as a team, I had indicated that I still wanted to play competitively. Meanwhile, Laine Peters, who had been our alternate during much of our run, talked to Kim about playing together, but only recreationally. Kim decided to do it and brought Nancy on board too, reinforcing that it would just be for fun. Mary-Anne and I had talked about playing together, but like the others she didn't want to play competitively. She joined them as the skip of the team.

Monty Mosher wrote a story about all of this that ran on the front page of *The Chronicle Herald*. I told him I was sort of shocked when the other three put the team together, and he asked if I was hurt by their decision. I had to say, the answer was yes. From the outside, it certainly looked bad, as if the team had left me. I had even said that playing for fun might be a good idea for me too, but Kim wasn't convinced I would be happy playing together without the competitive aspect. Truthfully, she was so right about that. Once we'd decided to break up the team, she didn't want any more of the intense stuff. What started as a conversation between a couple of the girls turned into something bigger, and none of it was planned that way. Kim describes it now as being like a marriage breakup, with a lot of miscommunication and misunderstanding. We were all feeling a little hurt at the end of what had been a long time together, and no one was thinking about how these decisions might affect each of us. I felt left out, but that was never their intention. I also had to accept that they maybe knew me better than I knew myself—I wouldn't be able to play for fun with the same group of people and switch off my competitiveness.

Once it became a front-page news story, things were even rougher. In Monty's article, Nancy was quoted as saying, "I can see where people would look at it and say that's a competitive team [meaning her and the other three]. We're going to play in some of the spiels because there really is no other forum for us to play, but it's going to be completely less disciplined. There will be fewer expectations. We just want to stay plugged into the sport without it being a complete priority." So, what had started as a recreational team was now going to be doing some competing. Stories surfaced that I was bitter that they had decided to go from playing for fun to trying to qualify for the provincial playdowns. Looking back on it now, Kim acknowledges that she should have

asked herself at the time if she was really going to be satis-
fied playing only for fun. We were all trying to figure out
what to do next, and that is a hard thing for any athlete, I
think. It became a bigger issue than it ever should have, and
I can see now why and how it all went down. It certainly
wasn't the media's fault—things just spiralled. The bottom
line is that through it all, we found a way to maintain our
friendships. It was certainly hard initially, but I think every
curler goes through this process in her curling career. All
teams dissolve at some point, and because our team had
done so much, our breakup was bigger than most.

In October, Kim's mom, Audrey, passed away—she had
been diagnosed with terminal cancer only two months
earlier—and this brought us all back together. Audrey was a
wonderful person and one of our biggest cheerleaders. She
introduced Kim to the game as a child and gave her the love
of the sport. Audrey's passing really opened our eyes. As Kim
says, life is sometimes bigger than the little things, and it was
silly what was happening to us. But it takes awhile to heal. We
started getting together for birthdays and would make a point
of having lunches together. We mended the fences and everything went back to the way it had been. We were sisters again.

When our team broke up, our working relationship with
Ken stopped as well. What he had done for us over all that
time was selfless and nothing short of amazing. He gave us
a lot of his time. When I needed mental therapy, he was
there—and he had to talk me off the ledge a lot. I don't know
if every skip in the world is as fragile as I am. When I'm
tough, I'm tough. But getting to tough from my starting
point, which is like a cracked egg, is no easy task. Until I got
on the ice I operated in fight-or-flight mode, and I'm sure I
was difficult to work with.

When my sister Monica heard about our team breaking up, she talked to me about joining her competitive team, skipped by my former teammate Kay Zinck. Monica played lead and Mary Mattatall played second, and they had an opening for a vice-skip. I had played with all of these women before, so I thought it was a nice option.

The team took some convincing, though. Everyone knew I had been playing as skip for a long time. Monica says it best: A curling team works well when everyone falls into the right position. Players come to love their position and own it. When everything runs along automatically that way, no one is thinking about playing any other spot. Kay is a good skip, and it wouldn't have made for a good team dynamic if I was always looking at her position instead of my own. But I wanted to play with them, and I wanted to play third. In the end, we all agreed to give it a try.

We had a decent year and it was fun playing together. Adjusting to playing vice-skip was harder than I'd thought it would be, though. While my teams were always a democracy, we had played together for so long that we always knew what the next move was. But, after having played on the same team for so long, I could feel it in my bones: The same magic wasn't there. We made it to the Nova Scotia provincial finals, but lost to Jill Mouzar's team.

FOR THE FOLLOWING 2007–2008 season, I decided I didn't want to play in the Provincials and focused instead on trying to qualify for the 2009 Canadian Olympic Curling Trials. The idea started when I was asked to fill in for Kelley Law, who was skipping a Vancouver-based team that included Georgina Wheatcroft, Darah Provencal, and Shannon Aleksic, in the season-ending 2007 Players' Championship in Calgary. That tournament is the final Grand Slam cashspiel of the season on the women's curling tour. Kelley couldn't play due to work commitments, so Georgina called me to fill in. We made it all the way to the semifinals before losing to Jennifer Jones. But I liked the way we played, and when Kelley decided to retire, Georgina and I talked about possibly keeping the team together. If we kept playing in the cashspiel circuit, we could earn enough points in the Canadian Team Ranking System to qualify for a spot in the 2009 Olympic Trials. Georgina is such a determined, focused player, and we decided to give this a go along with Darah Provencal. We added Kate Hamer, who had played with Sherry Middaugh, from Ontario.

So there I was back in it, or at least seriously dipping a toe in the waters, playing on a team with two players from British Columbia, one from Ontario, and one from Nova Scotia—a cross-Canada foursome. That had its drawbacks, though. I flew out to join them at tournaments, which was an unusual situation. And because we couldn't practise together, we didn't do well enough in the cashspiels to earn the points that would allow us to qualify for the Olympic Trials. Not practising together is a big problem for any team that wants to be successful. But I had gone into the season thinking it could work.

Mary-Anne, Kim, Laine, and Nancy continued to play together, and ended up winning the 2008 Nova Scotia Provincials to qualify for the Scotties. They'd barely curled together that season, but their sheer talent was such that they could show up at the Provincials and win. Mary-Anne had skipped before—she could play any position—and is a natural at it. At the Scotties, they beat some of the better teams in the tournament and finished the round robin with a 6–5 record, but didn't qualify for the playoffs. I sure missed not being there with them. When you look at the big picture, it's true that we had the hiccup of a difficult breakup, but overall the positives far outweigh everything else. And we all learned from that experience and grew from it.

IN 2011, something wonderful happened for all of us. The Nova Scotia Sport Hall of Fame inducted our whole group: Kim, Mary-Anne, Nancy, Mary Sue, Laine, Ken Bagnell, Peter Corkum (who had been our coach for many years), and myself. It was a night when we all got to savour together what we had accomplished. We shared a lot of stories with the crowd and it was fun. Bruce Rainnie, a sportscaster with the CBC and someone I had known and worked with for a long time, said we were probably the greatest team in Nova Scotia sports history. It was a night filled with lots of great memories, but most importantly it was so good to be back with my curling family. We had been through so much together over the years—births, deaths, winning, and losing—which pretty much cemented us together. Plus, we all love each other dearly.

It was such a treat to be recognized like that at home with this amazing group of people. We'd started a journey together with no idea of how far we would go, and there we were. We'd been all across Canada, and had seen a lot of the world. We'd beaten the odds and become more together than we could have on our own. Our run was truly over then, and all I could feel was gratitude for the incredible journey we had taken.

CHAPTER 9
TELLING STORIES

I love to tell stories, and I have been fortunate to do that for a living. For over thirty years now I've been a reporter, beginning with private radio and then moving to the Canadian Broadcasting Corporation. With the CBC, I've been lucky enough to get some wonderful assignments.

My favourite assignment is always the Olympics. They are The Show. I've been fortunate to cover nine Olympics in all, which have taken me to Asia, Russia, Europe, and North America. Whenever I'd get the call that I was going to be part of CBC's coverage, I'd be so excited. I remember getting that first call from CBC's Bob Moir in 1988, asking if I wanted to be part of the team for the Summer Games in South Korea. I probably responded coolly with "Yeah, of course." But when I hung up the phone, I'm pretty sure I screamed with excitement. It's such an honour. I was assigned to work on features about South Korea that would air during Olympic coverage, and flew from Halifax to CBC's headquarters in Toronto to begin preparation. We travelled to Seoul three weeks before the Games to shoot the stories. In addition to covering the actual Olympic Games, CBC wanted to tell stories about the region and people to give viewers a feeling of where the Games were taking place.

Going to South Korea for the first time and experiencing that as a broadcaster was jaw-dropping. I knew I was a rookie and needed to watch and listen to those with more experience. One thing I learned: A lot goes on behind the scenes to deliver all of the magical Olympic moments. From finding guests, to shooting the elements for the story, to making a shot list, writing, and then editing; easily ten hours would go into each two-minute feature.

Of course, the biggest story of the 1988 Olympics was Canada's Ben Johnson running in the finals of the 100-metre dash. CBC's Don Wittman, whom I worked with on curling coverage, called the race, and it was epic. Lots of drama and hype led up to the showdown between Johnson and his American rival, Carl Lewis, winner of nine Olympic Gold medals and eight World Track and Field gold medals. Johnson won easily in a record time of 9.79 seconds. But the sheer joy of watching him win was short lived, as it was quickly followed by shock and pandemonium when Johnson tested positive for steroids and was stripped of the gold medal by the International Olympic Committee (IOC). A global media frenzy ensued, with everyone trying to find a different way to tell the story of the disgraced Canadian superstar who had won the glamour event at the Games. I was assigned to do man-on-the-street interviews—or streeters, as they are called in the business—to ask people what they thought of Ben Johnson's fall from grace.

Because we wore CBC jackets with the CBC logo and Canadian flag, we were often asked about Johnson. The local people would point at us and say in broken English, "Ben Johnson ... bad." There had been numerous scandals before at the Olympics, but the fall of the 100-metre king introduced everyone to the issue of doping in sport.

Being a relative rookie broadcaster, it was interesting to see the coverage and the way in which both network news and sports teams worked so hard to cover a huge story that was changing by the minute. Other than doing streeters, I was not a part of the coverage, but I was able to watch in the wings as the reporters and producers worked to keep advancing the story. As my first Olympics broadcast, it was a barnburner. I naively went into those Games believing the conventional wisdom that the Olympics are all about that famous motto "Citius, Altius, Fortius" (or Faster, Higher, Stronger), but many of us returned home a little jaded about the Olympic Movement.

I was thrilled in 1992 to get the call again to go to the Winter Games in Albertville, France. I had missed the 1988 Winter Games in Calgary, as CTV had the broadcast rights that year. As in those Games, in 1992 curling was still a demonstration sport and hoping to get full-medal status. Unlike for the previous Winter Games, though, this time there were no Olympic Trials. Rather, the Canadian Curling Association chose the 1991 Brier winner (Kevin Martin of Edmonton) and Scotties winner (Julie Skinner of Vancouver). I provided curling coverage along with Don Duguid, and the venue was in a beautiful Alpine town well outside of Albertville called Pralognan-la-Vanoise. It felt like we were in a bit of a vacuum, far away from the rest of the Olympics action. What stood out the most was that the venue suffered an ice-plant breakdown and wound up having only two playable sheets. The other two sheets had pools of water on them. To squeeze in all of the games, the schedule had to be rearranged and we ended up covering curling from the crack of dawn till midnight. The two functional sheets of ice were less than perfect, too. Julie's team pulled off a bronze medal, while Kevin's team placed fourth. So, curling at those 1992 Olympics was marred by dismal attendance and melting ice. But that wouldn't deter the IOC from eventually voting curling in as a full-medal sport for the 1998 Olympics in Japan.

The Canadian Curling Association and the World Curling Federation had worked to raise the profile of the game and increase the number of countries playing the sport. Also, at least in Canada, curling was drawing significant TV ratings. So, the IOC decided that curling belonged as a full-medal sport in the Winter Games. It was a big moment for the sport, because for two weeks every four years the world stops and watches the Games. This would be an opportunity to display the sport, still primarily a Canadian obsession, to a bigger television audience. For me, personally, given that the year was 1992, the news that curling was going to be a full-medal Olympic sport by 1998 made me feel like I had missed the Olympic boat; 1998 seemed a lifetime away. But as a broadcaster, I was excited that curling had arrived. It had actually been an Olympic sport in 1924 and a demonstration sport in 1932, but the sport had changed so much since then.

THE FOLLOWING YEAR, in 1993, my life and career took a nice turn. Luke was born, and that added a lot of joy, fun, and chaos to our lives. He jumped right into the action—two days after coming home he was already part of our crazy schedules, making a trip to the arena in Mom's taxi (every mother's car is one) to get Zach to his hockey game—and he hasn't slowed down since. A few months after Luke was born, I switched from working with local CBC news to the twenty-four-hour CBC Newsworld. I started doing weather and sports for the national morning show. While sports were my background, doing the weather was something new for me. What I didn't know was that becoming the "weather girl" on Newsworld would upstage my role broadcasting sports. While a lot of people love sports, Canadians really love to talk about the weather all the time.

I've done the weather from Portage and Main in Winnipeg when it was minus-thirty, and I've done it from Iqaluit when it was minus-forty. I've stood outside and done the weather in Halifax during hundred-millimetre rainstorms, and I've done it from the top of Signal Hill in St. John's with one-hundred-kilometre-per-hour winds. Maybe that doesn't sound very fun, but the best part of reporting the weather was getting out of the studio and being in the elements.

While I wasn't a meteorologist, covering the weather wasn't a big stretch for me. For starters, I'd always been in tune with the weather. As a kid who sailed and biked all the time, knowing the weather was important; in Nova Scotia, the weather changes so quickly, you have to pay attention. I've always been in tune with sunrise and sunset, high tides, low tides, everything.

In broadcasting, it is easy to get pigeonholed, so after reporting on sports for eleven years, the idea of a change yet still keeping the sportscasting was exciting. Plus, moving to CBC Newsworld allowed me to break into this new world of twenty-four-hour news. At the time, the idea of "news around the clock" was still novel. CNN began in 1980 and CBC launched Newsworld in 1989 (it is now called CBC News Network), so in 1993, when I started with them, it was an exciting time to be part of something new.

When it came to reporting the weather, I had a good role model. I grew up watching a guy named Rube Hornstein, a trained meteorologist who worked as the very first weatherman for the CBC in Halifax. He reported the weather from 1954 until he retired in 1981, and he was a star in the city. Rube had one of those high-tech (at least at the time) chalkboards. He would draw a map of Canada on one side and then flip it around and have a map of Nova Scotia on the other side. Using his chalk, he'd write in the numbers and talk about low-pressure systems and frontal systems. It wasn't quite the green-screen technology we use today, but Rube was a legend.

Coincidentally, Rube Hornstein went to my church. Everyone there knew Rube as a famous weatherman, and he had the most beautiful speaking voice a person could have. So, his volunteer job at church was training the altar readers. I signed up and he taught me and the other readers how to enunciate, pause at the right time, make eye contact, and so on. I was only fourteen years old, but he was giving me valuable training for both my altar reading and my future broadcasting career. Rube was an old-school broadcaster. Compared to today's technology, his chalkboard seems primitive, but I'm willing to guess that Rube's forecasts were pretty reliable.

By the time I was doing the weather, the chalkboard was long gone, replaced by the green screen, which is television magic. It's common enough now, but when first introduced it was amazing. I stood in front of, literally, a green screen over which the graphics were superimposed. It's fun to use and takes some getting used to. And no green clothing is allowed or you disappear on camera.

The green screen gives the viewer the illusion that the weatherperson is actually in front of the screen with all of the images seen on TV. There are monitors on each side of the screen that I would look at to make sure I was pointing to the right place. And unlike doing the news or sports, where the script is running for us to read (called an auto-cue), weather reporters memorize the weather details and ad lib what they say.

My basic rule as a broadcaster is always to convey the story simply, especially in morning television before people have had their coffee. What information do they need to know? Is there a pile of snow or a big windstorm coming? I have just two minutes to deliver the message.

Since I wasn't a meteorologist when I started doing the weather, I visited Environment Canada and watched how they got their information. To me, reporting on the weather was no different than reporting on a sport I'd never played. I needed to sit and watch how it was done and become a mini-expert. The weather broadcast seems simple when it involves just providing the temperatures and indicating whether it will be a sunny or cloudy day. But it always seems that there's a storm system somewhere in Canada. When big storms were coming, I'd call Environment Canada and the meteorologist would break it down for me.

There were times I was sent to cover a storm or flood on-site, and three assignments stand out for me: Hurricane Juan in Halifax in 2003, the massive flood in Fredericton in 2008, and Hurricane Igor in Newfoundland and Labrador in 2010. In all three, the devastation was huge. There were millions of dollars in damage and people had no power for days; their basements were flooded and roads were impass-able. I remember doing one of my reports while paddling in a canoe on Water Street in Fredericton. Two days later, as the waters of the Saint John River continued to rise, the hotel we

were staying at—The Lord Beaverbrook—had to be evacu-
ated because water started gushing inside.

Severe storms such as these are so devastating to people
who live through them that the talk becomes less about
weather details (unless more bad weather is coming) and
more about the weather's impact on people's lives. People
become the face of the storm, and their personal losses and
struggles are the story.

Covering Hurricane Juan in Halifax was interesting
because, like so many people in the city, we had no power
for a week, which meant no hot water and that everything
in the fridge and freezer had to be thrown out. But our incon-
veniences were small compared to so many others who had
huge property damage from the massive trees that fell on
their homes. The damage throughout the city was wild. One
positive thing that came out of the storm was that people kept
having neighbourhood street parties, barbecuing together,
and neighbours helped others to clear and clean up fallen
trees. There was a constant symphony of chainsaws in Halifax
that week.

Covering a storm on-site requires a totally different mindset from broadcasting in the studio, because you are seeing
the damage first-hand. It's about finding out who's affected
and how. What's being done about the damage, and how are
people going to get help? As a reporter, you hope your stories
shine a light on what people are going through. The hope is
that your coverage will prompt a solution, whether that's the
Red Cross coming, the fire department rescuing people from
their homes, or even the army moving in to clear trees away
from houses.

When I first started reporting weather, I looked at it as an
extra on top of my sportscasting. But soon people started to

know me more as the "weather girl." I think a big part of that was that as a weather reporter I could inject more personality into what I was doing. Perhaps I became better known for doing the weather simply because people in Canada really pay attention to it. Every day, people get up and wonder what the weather will be like—it can vary so much, particularly in Atlantic Canada. There always seemed to be something important to discuss, so even though I started as a layperson, I worked to understand the weather better. The way television covers weather has definitely grown, but everything in television has grown exponentially with the rise of the five-hundred-channel universe. There are now dedicated networks for just about everything—things I thought would never work, such as HGTV, W Network, or World Fishing Network. And, of course, there's a weather network. I don't think I could have foreseen this evolution of television.

It felt strange becoming known as the "weather girl," because I was used to being called "the curler." No one had ever shouted out anything to me when I was a sportscaster, but weather resonated with people. I started receiving fan letters from viewers. I'd received letters before from curling fans, but I think as a weatherperson, people felt like I was their neighbour. (I suppose, in some cases, I actually was.) People would also send me knitted things, such as a hat to wear on air. One person sent me moose meat from Labrador because he thought I'd like it. I think it meant I was connecting with people, which is what every reporter wants. In a sense, you're being invited into someone's living room; you want them to think of you as someone who will sit down with them and have a coffee.

Allan Fotheringham wrote a story on the last page of *Maclean's* magazine about my job reporting the weather for CBC. I was a *Maclean's* fan, and liked Fotheringham's column at the back of every issue, so like a lot of people I always opened the magazine backwards. So, imagine my surprise when I opened that issue and saw a caricature of me accompanied by a full article. That was pretty cool.

I LOVED WORKING on the morning show, except for one thing—the hours. Ask anyone who works in morning television or radio and they'll tell you the big drawback is being up well before sunrise. I set the alarm for 4:30 a.m. and was ready for work an hour later. While people with "normal" jobs were waking up and getting ready to go to work, I'd already been hard at it.

THE BEST PART about broadcasting is getting out and meeting people, and going to new places I might never have seen otherwise. In 1996, I went to the Summer Olympics in Atlanta. Heat is something everyone has to deal with at the Summer Games, and "Hotlanta" was no different. There were misting stations everywhere to help people cool off. In 2000, Sydney was so hot that organizers were worried about the beach volleyball players burning their feet at Bondi Beach. Greece was hot in 2004, too. I can't remember covering a Summer Olympics in which it wasn't pretty damn hot. For me, though, the heat prize goes to the 2008 Games in Beijing. There, they were battling both heat and pollution. Organizers tried their best to manage the pollution by limiting car use and shutting down some factories, but every day you could still see a layer of grey.

However, the weather is a secondary story at the Olympics. The main story is the athletes, of course. Although there have been times where something happens that overshadows everything. In Atlanta, I was covering the Games for CBC Newsworld. My family came along on this trip and things were going well until that fateful night when the bombing took place at Centennial Olympic Park. It killed one person and injured many more, plus it cast a huge shadow on the Olympics in general. There was suddenly a fear that the incident could escalate into something bigger.

Scott and Zach were returning from watching a basketball game and had just left Centennial Olympic Park. The bomb went off shortly after they got on the train to come back to the hotel, so they were fine. I remember the call I received from Newsworld senior producer Mark Bulgutch to head over to the Olympic Stadium to do a live report. All events on the next day had been cancelled. Knowing that my family was safe, I wasn't concerned about my own safety, figuring the worst was over. Maybe that was naiveté on my part, but I wasn't alone in that thinking. We journalists have a tendency to think that nothing is going to happen to us. We were simply focused, scrambling to get information on the bombing and reactions to it from the athletes. Everything was being shut down because ensuring the safety of every Olympic site and, of course, the athletes was the top priority. We were all trying to get back to the broadcast centre or phoning people to report on what was happening where we were. It really was madness. There was a certain eeriness to the city, though, as I made my way to the Olympic Stadium, where I would be reporting—suddenly Atlanta was a ghost town. Even though security had been high at the Olympics since the 1972 tragedy in Munich, they amped it up even more after the bombing in Atlanta. Those Atlanta Olympics certainly stand out in my mind, in much the same way as the 1988 Seoul Games and the Ben Johnson doping scandal; at both Games, innocence was shattered.

Having said that, generally the Olympics feel safe because security is everywhere and it increases at every Games. Every venue is in its own locked-down zone. You get used to the bag searches, the metal detectors, and the body pat-downs. Still, making it through the hurdles of Olympic security should be its own medal sport.

There was one new medal sport shaping up for the following Winter Games—curling was finally getting its debut at the 1998 Olympics in Nagano, Japan. In 1997, the Canadian Curling Association revisited the system for qualifying for the Olympic Trials. This time around, they changed the format. There would be no more tryouts; rather, ten men's teams and ten women's teams would qualify through a process. The winning teams from the 1994 to 1997 Brier and Scott Tournament of Hearts were given immediate entry, while the remaining teams were decided by World Curling Tour cashspiels in four regions of the country. My team tried to qualify, but we didn't meet the standards.

The Trials took place in Brandon, Manitoba. Sandra Schmirler's reigning Canadian women's champion team from Regina won the ladies' side, while Mike Harris's team from Ontario won the men's. Both teams earned the right to represent Canada for the first time in medal competition. I wasn't at those Olympic Games, and I missed a spectacular debut for our sport. The Schmirler rink cemented their place as one of the greatest teams to ever play the game and won the gold medal. And the men's rink captured the silver medal. I was thrilled to watch it all from afar, back in Halifax, like so many other Canadians, realizing that curling had just taken a huge leap.

IT WAS AROUND this time that my curling team was enjoying some of its best years. The early 2000s were a whirlwind. We were at the top of our game, and training harder than ever. Between the Scotties and World competitions and all of the travelling I did to cover sports and weather, it was like I never stopped. But I loved every minute of it. Life at home was wonderful, too. Zach and Luke were growing up quickly and becoming amazing young adults. They must have inherited their love of sports from Scott and me, because they both have done very well.

In 2009, I moved to Toronto temporarily with Luke. He was spending the year training at the Ace Tennis Academy, and I continued to do weather and sports, commuting from Burlington, just west of the city, to the CBC's office on Front Street in downtown Toronto. Luke's dream was to play university tennis in the United States, and he felt the increased competition, training, and coaching would help him accomplish that goal. He was only going into grade nine and made very persuasive arguments to me and Scott about why we should make this happen. It didn't take long to agree since I more than recognized that fire in his eyes. Next thing we knew, we were packing up the car and driving to southern Ontario and renting an apartment in Burlington. Scott stayed home and manned the house; Zach was studying at Dalhousie University but actually doing a transfer year in Salamanca, Spain, so the timing worked out well—aside from the fact I had to wake up at 3:30 a.m. to give myself extra time to travel. Toronto is considerably larger than Halifax. In Halifax, to get from my house to the CBC took ten minutes. Travelling from Burlington to the CBC took an hour by car. It was much more demanding on my system doing the job there—I was drinking lots of good coffee to be up and ready and on air by 6 a.m.

And Luke was thriving in this new competitive environment. The year was like a big adventure for us.

As it turns out, that would be my last year reporting the weather and sports. In October 2009, the CBC decided to use meteorologists for weather and to do sports out of Toronto. Luke and I were moving back to Halifax, so I was done as the "weather girl" but ready for whatever would come next.

The next thing turned out to be a gift from the universe. My assignment was human interest stories, which meant I was returning to my reporting roots. I had been looking for a new challenge anyway, as I had been slipping into automatic pilot a bit in my weather and sports role. It was time for a change, and the new work opened up a whole other part of my brain. I love to challenge myself, and learning a new kind of reporting made me feel that old excitement again.

People and the things they do are fascinating to me, so the broad umbrella of human interest stories was perfect. I was a bit out of practice with field reporting, compared to being in the studio, so I had to go back and remember everything I'd learned as a rookie reporter. There's a lot of leg work to be done in reporting, from finding the story, to setting up your guests, to getting all of the elements for the shot. Then you make a shot list, write, and edit. Each story is labour intensive. But it's been fun, and I certainly don't miss the 3 a.m. wake-up calls!

There is never a shortage of stories to tell. One time I did a story about a woman who makes art out of shoes—she blew my mind. She was able to take a pair of shoes and transform it into art, and each piece was amazing. Another time I did a story about Doris Stephens, who wanted to go for a ride in a vintage airplane on her 102nd birthday. Her joy for life was so inspiring. Recently, I reported the story of a ninety-three-year-old man who wanted to do a tandem sky dive to raise money for Gander Heritage Memorial Park in Newfoundland. It was his first time jumping out of an airplane. I think I'm drawn to people whose passion and joy are so obvious they're contagious. People are doing incredibly interesting things every day, and I love watching and sharing these stories. It always makes me go "wow." After my meningitis scare, my goal was to live with joy and gratitude, so I love to surround myself with people who are living examples of that.

We use a team approach in our Halifax newsroom, and I'm lucky that our assignment editor, Jamie Lipsit, knows the kinds of stories that are in my wheelhouse and the producers encourage my style. I also enjoy digging up good stories myself. The more I get out in the community, the more stories fall in my lap. People sometimes write to me with story ideas they think will be perfect for me. And one story often leads to another. I did a story about a man who makes lamps out of bicycle parts, and then he told me about a retired couple who was building a seventy-five-foot schooner in their front yard and asked if I'd be interested in covering that. I was thinking, *A real-life Noah's Ark? Point me in the right direction!* It turned out that they were an amazing couple. Warren and Andrea Manthorne live in a land-locked area of Nova Scotia called Upper Onslow. Their labour of love is a schooner called the *Lena Blanche* that they are building by themselves. It is a huge and beautiful project, and when they finish they plan to teach themselves how to sail. Their work and dedication to it was so impressive.

When I work on these stories, I always want to get right in there, talking to people and getting as close to the action as I can. They're called reporter involvement stories, and I prefer this approach because I think it helps viewers get a true feel for the stories I am telling. I have done three Polar Bear Swims, jumped out of an airplane, and rappelled down two buildings. I've bungee jumped in New Zealand, zip-lined a river in China, learned to play underwater hockey, surfed, kitesurfed, eaten scorpions, and wrapped myself in a boa constrictor all in the name of a fun story. And it has definitely been fun.

To do a reporter involvement story, you have to jump in with both feet—literally and figuratively. That level of commitment and fun shows through in the final piece, and it sets the reporting apart in this brand of storytelling. Whether riding a horse or milking a cow—whatever it is you're doing—you want to take the viewer with you.

My ultimate reporter involvement piece was telling my own story from the hospital when I had bacterial meningitis. It was called "Doctor Google." I had been preparing to do the shoot prior to getting sick, but suddenly I became the story. During my hospital stay, I was pumped full of steroids to bring the swelling down in my brain and it gave me incredible energy. So, I booked a medical specialist and a few other experts to discuss why it's dangerous to diagnose oneself on Google. I had gone online and diagnosed myself erroneously as having pleurisy—man, was I wrong. So there I was in a johnny gown in an isolated ward of the hospital doing an interview from my bed. This was maybe taking reporter involvement to the extreme, but the piece really worked because it showed just how far off I had been on my diagnosis, and the danger it had caused.

I WAS ENJOYING my new work with the CBC, but starting to be concerned that I wouldn't see the Olympic Games back at CBC again in my career. The CBC had been outbid for the 2010 Winter Olympics in Vancouver and the 2012 Summer Olympics in London. Luckily, CBC got back into it to cover the 2014 Winter Games in Sochi. It's not impossible to cover an event like the Olympics without holding the broadcasting rights, but without them journalists are very restricted. Only employees of companies with broadcasting rights are allowed to do interviews from the events as they are happening. Without that access, it's difficult to do the job well and experience the emotions of the athletes, coaches, family, and anyone else connected with the teams. Of course I'm biased, but I think no one covers the Olympics better than CBC. From the opening theme, to the scenic, to the features, and then the sports themselves, the way CBC covers the Games and Canadian athletes has always given me a tremendous sense of pride.

In Sochi, I was assigned to cover curling as well as some human interest stories. My favourite was the story I did about vodka in Russia. What beer is to Canada, vodka is to Russia. Until you've been to a Russian grocery store, with its row upon row of vodka, you have no idea just how many different brands there are. I also did stories from Canada Olympic House, where the Canadian athletes and their families relax, and outside at some unexpected locales. These made me feel like I'd contributed something beyond the Games.

I've always joked that the Olympics is the ultimate reality show. The International Olympic Committee calls the shots, and the entire event is well orchestrated. I remember that a man fell from the stands during one of the curling games at the 2010 Winter Olympics in Vancouver. All of the curlers stopped playing, wondering if he was okay—he made quite a thud—but the cameras of the host feed never shifted, because that wasn't part of the show. In television, we all learn to discuss only what's on the screen. You don't want to confuse the picture the audience is seeing by saying, "You're not going to believe what just happened," because they're not seeing that part of the story. When everybody stopped curling, the news instinct to discuss what had just happened kicked in, but the Olympics is about the show, and what the IOC wants the worldwide audience to see is brought to you by major sponsors. A fan falling is not part of that.

That year in Vancouver, I was reporting for NBC since CBC did not have the broadcast rights. I was fortunate enough to be able to take a leave of absence from the CBC to work for the Americans, and it proved to be a great experience. First off, the fans in Vancouver were amazing, and everywhere you went you saw a sea of Team Canada clothing. Plus, Team Canada really did own the podium that year. But I was working for an American network. They brought all of their production and broadcasting personnel together for a meeting just before the Games began. Dick Ebersol, NBC's head of sports, hosted that meeting and it was a who's who of talent, including Bob Costas, Mary Carillo, and Cris Collinsworth—broadcasting superstars—and all of their analysts. There were world champions and Olympians from every sport. My jaw dropped walking into that room with all that talent. The meeting was a reminder about how to cover sports for television, letting the pictures and sound speak to allow the moment to shine, avoiding being a cheer-leader—all those kinds of things. I didn't know any of the NBC personnel, but it was a neat experience. I found that stepping out of my routine with the people I was accustomed to working with gave me fresh ideas and re-energized me.

There were some familiar faces in that room, too. Those Olympics reunited me with Don Duguid, the first time we had been part of the same broadcasting team since 1997. We worked with Andrew Catalon, in his first stint broadcasting the sport and doing play-by-play duties. Working with Don was like putting on a comfortable pair of shoes. The rhythm was there. We were in the booth together—as opposed to me standing at ice level, which isn't allowed in the Olympics—and it's easier to work that way because we could see the visual cues the other person was getting ready to discuss, or use the telestrator, that gizmo that allows you to draw on the screen to show what you think will happen on a certain shot or play. Stars such as Donald Sutherland and Wayne Gretzky attended the curling event. Canadian prime minister Stephen Harper attended the men's and women's finals, both of which featured Canadian teams. Canada was well represented with teams skipped by Edmonton's Kevin Martin and Calgary's Cheryl Bernard. They collectively rocked that place. The curling venue was a really happening place to be, with lots of energy in the building. We had Gretzky in the broadcast booth with us for two ends of curling, and it was a treat because he seemed to really love the game and tried hard to understand the strategy. He was relaxed and having fun, a totally different vibe from the times I've interviewed him about hockey when his attitude is definitely more serious and his words are chosen more carefully. I might have been working for NBC during those games, but it took extra effort to stay neutral while covering Canada in both the men's and women's gold-medal games. Bernard lost a heartbreaker to Anette Norberg, to earn the silver medal for Canada, while Martin's rink was dominant in clinching the gold medal.

Wherever I've gone for the Olympics, I've tried to explore the host city beyond the events. In Beijing, I bought a bike—and got lost quite a few times trying to pedal from the International Broadcast Centre to our media hotel. In Sydney, I had a scooter to avoid the long wait for trains. I rented a bike in Vancouver for the 2010 Games and brought my own bike to Sochi, Russia, for the 2014 Games. But mostly, I like to walk. When you walk or bike, as opposed to when you take transit, you tend to really see a place. Making my own way around, I'm forced to figure out the streets and ask locals for help when I can't find my way. In Sochi, things were set up so the broadcast centre and the five venues were close together, which made it easy to bike. I felt I really saw Sochi as a result of biking to the broadcast centre each day.

As much as I like getting around on my own, there can be issues getting to and from events. There is a media shuttle that moves people around, but everyone is responsible for figuring out the venues and how to get to them. That media shuttle is far from perfect, and it is not unusual to hear stories of media buses getting lost. Sometimes we'd take a media bus to one spot and a subway to another. Even though we're provided with maps, navigating them can be like an Olympic sport for reporters. By the time I have it all figured out, it's just about time to board the plane to go home. Sochi was definitely the easiest for getting around, because of how Russia built the infrastructure for those Games. Of course, that came with a big price tag. The Sochi Games cost a staggering $50 billion.

At the Olympics, your job is to tell the athletes' stories, but access to them is limited, even for Olympics broadcast rights holders. We get first dibs, but the athletes are paraded down a cattle pen and every television reporter gets a whopping one minute with each athlete before he or she is pushed along to the reporter from the next country. After the athletes finish with television interviews, they move over to the print media. All anyone is hoping to get in that one minute, maybe two minutes if you are lucky, is a magical quote.

The Olympics, as fans know everywhere, provide so many spectacular moments. But the stories that give me chills are those of the athletes who work so hard to get there and don't win medals. Their sacrifices inspire me. While I never got to go to the Olympics as a curler, the broadcasting side of the Games is impressive. There are so many talented men and women in front of the cameras and behind the scenes who work together to broadcast the events and take great pride in what they do. This is their chance to shine and to make everyone feel as if they are right there at the Games with them. I never got to compete myself, but I'm so grateful to have been a part of telling Olympic stories.

I feel the same about other events, too. I loved covering the Commonwealth Games in both New Zealand and Victoria, British Columbia. And I always enjoyed reporting from the Canada Games, because they were my first big event as a competitor. Plus, when I covered the 2015 Canada Winter Games in Bathurst, New Brunswick, and the 2009 Canada Summer Games in Prince Edward Island, I got to report on my sons. Zach was at the Winter Games as the goaltender on the men's hockey team, and Luke was at the Summer Games on the Nova Scotia tennis team. That was pretty cool.

AS A REPORTER, you're sharing stories with an audience you never see, but you become part of people's lives because you are the conduit to what is happening in the world. I've always looked on being a reporter as an incredible privilege, and I've enjoyed every bit of the process. I feel fortunate to have been able to do different things in my career, and like so many other CBC employees, I love the place.

I've had several different jobs at the CBC and I continue to learn. The technology in the last five years has seen amazing changes, from shooting and viewing with your phone to Twitter. There are so many new platforms now compared to when I began in the early 1980s, when there were only radio, television, and print.

Television is changing quickly—all media, for that matter, are changing at a rapid pace—so it's important to keep adapting to new ways of reporting in the digital world. To think you can continue to do things the way you've always done them is naive. Change is something that occurs in every business. Throughout my broadcasting and curling careers, I have always tried to be aware of where things are going and how to move with them. Change, and adapting to it, is critical in my life as a curler, mother, and broadcaster.

CHAPTER 10
GETTING BACK IN THE GAME

It was a special treat to cover curling for NBC at the 2010 Winter Olympics in Vancouver. I got to see many of the women I had played against in my career, including Anette Norberg of Sweden, Debbie McCormick of the United States, Andrea Schöpp of Germany, Madeleine Dupont of Denmark, and Canada's Cheryl Bernard. While I loved reporting on the sport, being there ignited my desire to curl competitively again. It looked like such fun out there—intense, yes, but fun.

Once I started seriously thinking about competing, I didn't have to wait long to hook up with a team that needed a skip. Heather Smith, who'd played in the Scotties in 2000 as a third for my former teammate Kay Zinck and skipped her own team in 2004, had an opening on her squad. Jill Mouzar, who threw fourth stones, was moving to Toronto in the spring. The team, which included lead Teri Lake and second Blisse Comstock, immediately picked me as their first choice to be their skip because of my experience. Heather, who also curls out of the Mayflower Curling Club, called to ask if I'd be interested in joining her team, so we met at the Armview

Restaurant just down the street from my home. It was all quite serendipitous. It's not every day that you have a chance to join an established team, particularly one from the same club, and it seemed like a good fit. When Heather and I chatted, we discovered the goals of the existing team members were the same as mine in terms of practising and putting in the time to win the Provincials and get to the Scotties. I had known Heather and all of the girls for a long time, so I knew what they could do. They had done all the work and were chomping at the bit. I felt they were all pretty steady, with room to grow, too. Heather was so passionate about wanting to take her game to the next level in every way, and that was still attractive to me, to keep doing the work. I'd spent my whole life putting in that work. It becomes a habit, something I'd look for in different areas of life. That's just part of what I love to do. And it came at the perfect time, right after the 2010 Olympics, when I had been in the broadcast booth thinking how much I wanted to get back into the game.

We trained individually, and once a week during the summer we would do something fun together, such as go to a yoga class or the gym. We were doing the work that teams need to do to bond and get stronger on the ice. It can be hard for a fourth person to join an established team, and everyone made me feel welcome. We all knew each other from the club, so that helped. We played some tournaments in the fall and were feeling good about our chances.

We had a practice scheduled on the day I got sick. When I missed the practice, Teri called the house and was told I was feeling under the weather. What an understatement! By that time, I was in the emergency room, probably having a spinal tap. When Heather learned what was going on, she visited me in the hospital. We talked about my recovery time and she asked if I'd be ready to curl in the qualifying competition leading up to the Provincials. I had to tell her I wouldn't be curling at all that season—doctor's orders. Also, given my health crisis, curling was the last thing on my mind. First, I was too weak to play. But also, the doctors had told me I would likely need surgery to fix the small hole that opened into my brain, which is how bacteria had been able to enter and cause my illness in the first place.

The team had to decide what to do: fold up or reshuffle things. It was too late for them to find another skip, but they didn't want to quit. It was decided that Heather would move into the skip spot, and they recruited the very talented former junior champion Danielle Parsons to take my spot. It turns out it was the right move, as they went on to win the Provincials. Both Heather and I believe that everything happens for a reason, and this was her moment to skip again. She was really dropped into a pressure cooker, but played brilliantly. Her husband at the time, Mark Dacey, a former Brier champion, was coaching our team, and he also did a great job of guiding everybody.

But, oh, how I *wanted* to curl. I'd been curling for most of my life. I'd played in my first Canadian finals in 1980 as a twenty-year-old. That's young. And then two years later, I won the national title. Curling was a part of me. I'd spent years—more years than even most other serious competitors—organizing my life around practices, training, and competitions. I slept, ate, and worked curling every day. I wondered if this was what Gordie Howe had felt like. Longevity like ours required an intensity that was not easy to let go of. Especially among female curlers, that level of intensity was rare.

I'd worked hard to try to balance my work and my family and maintain that intensity in curling. But after my health scare, life became about more than just a curling game. It became about taking the time to do what normal people do. I think a lot of curlers will tell you that their lives aren't totally normal. Life for a curler is very focused. It's very driven. It's time spent in the gym and at the rink. It's coaching and working with sports psychologists. And it's travelling to a lot of bonspiels. That's what you have to do to play at the elite level, especially with the amount of money available through tournaments, sponsorship, funding from Sport Canada through the carded athlete program, and the chance to play in the Olympics. That is the evolution of the game from when I first began playing. The opportunities have grown so much over the years as the sport has developed.

I celebrated my fifty-first birthday on December 16, 2010, and it took on added meaning because of the meningitis. On that birthday, I was filled with gratitude that I was still alive. We celebrated as a family, going out for dinner at a Greek restaurant. I had been released from the hospital a few days before and was still on various drugs. The Victorian Order of Nurses, or VON, were coming to the house twice a day to administer drugs and check on me. I still wasn't 100 percent, but a birthday bash was in order.

When we came home from the restaurant, Scott and the boys had a massive cake waiting for me. We sang "Happy Birthday" and took the annual photo of me cutting the cake (a family tradition). Zach says it looks like all the others from previous birthdays, but I felt more alive and happy than any other year.

After the meningitis scare, I didn't think I'd ever curl at the Scotties again. I only wanted to play senior curling (being over fifty, I was now eligible), which is not as demanding. I didn't want to be a slave to the daily practices and constant weekend tournament grind anymore. I wanted to sip tea when I wanted, go to yoga when I felt like it, and take the dog for long walks on a whim. Senior curling would allow me to keep my hand in the sport I love, with the friends who mean a lot to me.

Once I was on the mend, and had the doctors' okay, I put together a Seniors team that included Nancy Delahunt, Marsha Sobey, and my sister-in-law Sally Saunders. I started curling again only about two or three weeks before the provincial Seniors competition, and I had to work hard to regain my strength. After lying in bed for so long, both in the hospital and at home on bedrest, your muscles start to atrophy quickly. On top of that, I was used to training every day. When I could finally start going for walks—an important part of the healing—doing that felt so healthy and perfect. Soon I could get back to work and then back to curling and feel that kind of normalcy. My first slide on the ice was an important step, and made it seem as if everything was going to be okay.

SOME ELITE CURLERS who have competed and won at the Brier or the Scotties will tell you that they'll never play at the Seniors level. It's a totally different experience, like going back to junior curling in terms of the atmosphere. The dynamics are similar—there are good teams and bad teams; some people make mistakes and some don't. But it's certainly different. You don't play in an arena. You play in a club and tournaments are not televised. When I first walked into the club for the competition, I quickly realized it wasn't what I was used to. It was definitely an adjustment, but it was still curling. I absolutely loved being on the ice, regardless of my age or the setting. I still felt the thrill of competition. I've always said I could be playing tiddlywinks for a toaster or a turkey and I'd still be competitive, no different from when I was a teenager. The rewards weren't the same at the Seniors level, but that didn't matter. Senior curling allows us to sit back, have a glass of wine, and curl with friends, yet when we get on the ice we still have that killer instinct.

Our team played well together and we won the Nova Scotia Senior Women's Provincials. I think I celebrated this more than winning the Scotties, given all I had been through. We moved on to the Canadian Senior Curling Championships in Digby, about three hours outside of Halifax. Digby is a tiny town in a fishing community with a view of the ocean that makes you swoon. The organizing committee did a wonderful job hosting it. We played solidly, but a few things were happening behind the scenes. First, Nancy's back went out mid-week, so we had to bring in an alternate. Alternates have it tough, coming into a tournament like that, but ours played great. But it's hard for me to not be on the ice with my wingman. I rely on Nancy a lot.

Also, there was another source of anxiety: my cerebral spinal fluid started leaking again. It interrupted my sleep, making me feel lethargic. When I had left the hospital in December, there was a slight hope I wouldn't need surgery to correct the problem. The doctors could see I had a small hole in my dura that was causing the cerebral spinal fluid to leak out, but they hoped that because of the swelling that happens during bacterial meningitis, the hole might have disappeared. My neurologist had told me to call him if the problem reoccurred. With fluid leaking from my nose again, I made the call. Yes, I continued curling, because I operate under the guiding principle that I'm bulletproof, but I was now bound for surgery.

Meanwhile, Heather Smith skipped her team to a win at the Provincials, and two days before the team left for the Scotties we had a meeting organized by Mark Dacey at my house. Even though I wasn't going to be going with them, I was still excited to help get them ready for the event. After winning the 2004 Brier as a skip, Mark knew how to win. We sat down and talked about the Scotties, how to break down the week with the kind of goal setting needed to be successful. Blisse and Danielle were first-year Scotties participants, so hearing from Mark and me hopefully helped them a lot. They were a solidly coached team. During the Scotties, I was in touch with Mark every night about who the team would play the next day and what I knew about them, how to approach them, and different things like that. I was happy to mentor in whatever way I could. I felt like I'd left them in the lurch, but it was pretty clear to me, especially after they won the Provincials and looked solid, that they were just fine without me. But if I could give them any advice along the way, I was happy to be their biggest supporter.

Perhaps surprisingly, it wasn't frustrating for me to watch them play. I had just come out of a life-and-death situation and was preparing for surgery. I knew I had a much bigger fight on my hands in terms of dealing with my own health and making sure I was well. I was on a whole other path. My priorities became clear and I didn't have any "I wish I was there" moments. I felt they had done really well without me, and I'd had a mentoring hand. We were a team that had worked together through the summer and fall, going to bonspiels. We had laid the groundwork and I watched them with a lot of interest. The team had a great run at the Scotties, finishing third. Heather was fabulous. She is a really confident, workaholic player, and I've always admired that in her. In the face of a lot of adversity, I thought they did an awesome job.

Meanwhile, I was getting ready for—and it seems odd even now to say it—brain surgery. It would involve an ear, nose, and throat doctor and a neurologist. The surgery is called endoscopic CSF leak repair, in which they go up through the nose, drill a bit, grab a patch of skin from your quadriceps muscle, and patch the hole. It's the ultimate plumbing job to stop a leak. It took about seven hours for the doctors to complete the surgery, and about four full months for me to recover. Then I was as good as new. I'm forever grateful to my spectacular surgeons, especially the wonderful Dr. David Clarke, who heads Neurosurgery at our Capital Health.

IN THE NEXT SEASON, 2011–2012, Nancy, Marsha, Sally, and I were raring to go after the provincial Seniors title again. To help prepare, we played in the International Bernese Ladies Cup bonspiel in Bern, Switzerland. It was a long way to travel, but a perfect place to go. We curled, but also had a great day skiing in the gorgeous Alps, tobogganing down the run in Grindelwald, drinking wine, and eating lots of cheese fondue. I suppose we were there more as tourists than as curlers. I hadn't skied much since first being in Switzerland for the World Championships in Geneva thirty years earlier. Skiing always conflicted with my curling schedule. Plus, I'm not much of a skier; I can get down a hill and I enjoy it, but I'm far from graceful. Back when I was a part of Team Canada, the Bernese Cup was an event we played at a few times, so it was familiar. All of the top international teams were there and it was great to see them all again, but we were really in over our heads at this competition.

Soon after returning from Switzerland, we played in the Nova Scotia Women's Senior Championships. We made it to the finals and played Colleen Pinkney's talented team that had won the World Seniors in 2010. It was a tough game, one that went back and forth, and we were lucky to be on top at the end of it. With that win, we were off to the Canadian Seniors in Abbotsford, British Columbia. We had a solid event, but wound up finishing third, losing out in the semifinals to Cathy Cunningham of Newfoundland and Labrador. They then lost to Cathy King of Alberta in the finals. I had faced both Cathys numerous times in the Scotties, and that is the cool thing about senior curling. It's a way for everyone to stay connected. To think that Cathy King and I first played against each other as junior players, and there we were over thirty years later, still throwing rocks at houses.

The 2012 curling season was done for us, but I had my health and no shortage of energy. That summer, Scott and I biked across France on a one-thousand-kilometre journey. It was a trip I'd wanted to make since 1984, but there was never enough time what with work, curling, and then starting a family. After bacterial meningitis, a trip to France with my husband—cycling and seeing the countryside and the Alps, and drinking some wine—became a priority.

I was feeling great, and I had begun to think I was quite done with the Scotties by this point in my curling career. But then I got a call from my former teammate Mary-Anne Arsenault. She had an opening on her roster and was trying to get to the Scotties, with an outside hope of also getting to the 2013 Olympic Trials in December. In addition to at least a top-three finish at the Scotties, we would need a good chunk of World Curling Tour points—they factor in the Canadian Team Ranking System, which places value on various tournaments. If we had enough points, we would qualify for the Pre-Trials, a twelve-team, triple knockout tournament in which the top two men's and women's squads qualify for the Trials, known as the Tim Hortons Roar of the Rings since 2005. The winning men's and women's teams at the Trials represent Canada at the Olympics. It was going to take a miracle for us to qualify for the Trials, but I can tell you that every curler across the country dreams that he or she may one day be part of the teams representing Canada at the Olympics. It had certainly been my dream more than once, and that was our goal.

It was Nancy who had put the bug in Mary-Anne's ear to give me a call, and I couldn't have been more excited to reconnect, try another position, and get back to the competitive cycle. Mary-Anne planned to continue skipping and needed to be convinced that I didn't want to be in control of the team and didn't want to skip. I wasn't interested in skipping, because I didn't want that pressure. I was seeing things differently now.

While Mary-Anne was thinking about it, she kept noticing me around town. Apparently, I even cut her off in traffic one time! Mary-Anne and I both believe in omens, and we figured the universe wanted us back together. Nancy no longer had the desire to commit to playing at that level, but luckily for us she came on board as our fifth and assumed a take-charge, directional role on the team. She really helped so much in making sure the team worked together. While some people in the curling world might have been surprised we reunited, Ken Bagnell, our mental coach throughout our glory years, wasn't one of them. He knew that in our hearts we were all sisters.

It was a little like *The Blues Brothers*, with Jake Blues (John Belushi) and his brother Elwood (Dan Aykroyd) reuniting their band one final time, on a mission. That's what it felt like—getting the band back together. In our case, it was a team of curlers.

The new team had Mary-Anne skipping, me playing third, Kim Kelly throwing second stones, and Jennifer Baxter playing lead. Jenn had played second for several years with Mary-Anne skipping, and dropped down to lead when Kim joined the team in the 2011–2012 season. Kim hadn't planned on playing competitively again, but when Mary-Anne made the decision to invite me to play third, Kim was keen.

In many ways, Nancy was the catalyst for this team. She instinctively knew what was needed to up the ante. Mary-Anne had what it took, but Nancy felt that I could bring a competitive edge to the team, even if I wasn't calling the shots. Because the team was coming together so late in the season, we wouldn't have the chance to build ourselves up as a team needs to. Trying to get to the top in just a few months was no small task.

I've always enjoyed the process of trying to get better and I love being part of a team, so it was fun being back together. But there was something special and cool about this squad coming full circle and being back on the ice together in new roles. Things were progressing, but the big change came in November at a huge bonspiel in Brantford, Ontario. All of the top teams were there, and there was a lot of money on the line and points that would go toward the Canadian Team Ranking System. But we weren't performing well as a team; I could feel it in my bones. And we didn't have the luxury of waiting for that magical team synergy to come along. We had lost a game and I went to bed looking for answers, wondering what we needed to do to get on track. The next morning, I awoke with the answer: I had to move from third to second. I didn't know if shaking up the lineup would help, but we needed to do something. I went downstairs for breakfast, and Mary-Anne and Kim were already up, so I told them about my epiphany. Mary-Anne had been used to Kim playing third from the previous season, and Kim, although she had played second years earlier, had more or less been a lifetime third. Second was the position where I'd started my curling life as a teenager. I didn't feel like I had been playing well enough at third. Plus, I'm a natural hitter, and I realized I could be more valuable in that spot. So it all made sense, and we switched positions. While we didn't have success right away, it would come later.

Playing second was a complete turnaround for me from my career as a skip. Skipping is a lonely position. You are separated from your teammates, in the house calling the game. And if you watch skips, they always look like the weight of the world is on their shoulders. At second, curlers are gabbing with their teammates and busy sweeping; it's a totally different vibe. I liked the new role and embraced the challenge of trying to do it well, which was not easy. It seemed to be the right move for the team, but I also wanted to see if I could learn some new tricks at that point in my career.

YOU COULD FEEL the energy on the team shift once we made the lineup change. I think in some ways Canadian teams have to be more like European teams that switch positions, sometimes in the course of a tournament. I've seen teams do five-person rotations that Canadian teams generally won't do unless there's an illness or some need to give the fifth some playing time. We knew we were in for a one-year commitment, and were feeling desperation to do whatever it took to win.

Things finally started coming together before the Provincials when we travelled back to the Bernese Cup in Switzerland. We won our four round robin games and defeated two-time Olympic champion Anette Norberg of Sweden in the opening round of the playoffs. We lost our next two games, but felt good about making it to the final four in a quality international field. We felt like we were hitting our stride.

Up next were the Nova Scotia Provincials. We knew we needed to win these and have a great Scotties in order to qualify for the Olympic Pre-Trials. We started strong, winning our first four games before losing 5–3 to Heather Smith, who was the defending champion and looking to win her third consecutive title. But we rebounded to win our remaining games and finished tied for first at 6–1 with Jocelyn Nix of the Glooscap Curling Club. Because we had beaten her team 9–1 in head-to-head play, we advanced straight to the finals. Jocelyn beat Heather 6–3 in their semifinals game, so it was our team against Jocelyn's in the finals.

It was a well-matched game. We started off slowly, with Jocelyn stealing the first two ends, but evened it out with single points in the third and fourth ends. Jocelyn took one in the fifth to lead 3–2 at the break. In the ninth end, the score was tied at four each. That's when the turning point came. We stole a pair to take control, and in the tenth Mary-Anne shot a pistol with her first stone, a double takeout, leaving them with only one stone and needing two points to win. In curling parlance, we ran them out of rocks and won 6–4.

The tears started to flow immediately, because we were going back to the Scotties. It would be the twenty-first time for me, the sixteenth for Kim, the eleventh for Mary-Anne, and the first for Jennifer. It was such an unbelievable thrill,

because it had been so long since I had been to the Scotties—
The Show; I could almost compare it to winning my first
Provincials in 1979. Every other Provincials win was exciting, but not nearly as much as the first. Now, making it back
to the Scotties seven years after I had last been there—I
couldn't wipe the smile off my face. I was so excited to get
that opportunity, particularly with fresh memories of lying in
a hospital in the fetal position only a couple of years earlier.
I had been through a lot and never thought I would ever
make it back again. Curling is a crazy game where anything
can happen. It was an unbelievably sweet moment. We had
one more big tournament to play—it seemed like the rightful
ending for all of us.

THE 2013 SCOTTIES took place in Kingston, Ontario, and
included a stellar field that featured many top teams. Playing
that year was reigning Canadian women's champion Heather
Nedohin and her team from Edmonton, previous Canadian
women's champions Jennifer Jones of Manitoba and Kelly
Scott of British Columbia, and former Canadian junior
champions Suzanne Birt (née Gaudet) of Prince Edward
Island and Rachel Homan of Ontario. Rachel was playing in
just her second Scotties and was having a great season,
going undefeated in her provincial playdowns. At the age of
twenty-three, she reminded me so much of myself at that
age, with her passion for the game.

Kim felt the same as I did, that it was really rewarding
to win the Provincials because we had worked so hard,
put in the effort, and had the energy. When she and I stepped
into the K-Rock Centre in Kingston, we both stood at the
edge of the sheets for the first practice, looking around and
soaking in the feeling. In her words, it felt so "homey, so

comfortable." It was an appreciation of being back in that environment, something we thought we'd never experience again. It had been five years for her and Mary-Anne and seven years for me. Nancy, as our fifth, was on the ice with us, too. With everything the four of us had been through over the decades, it was amazing to be back on the ice for those opening ceremonies.

Our team received tremendous warmth, affection, and support from the crowds, because many people were happy to see us back. We signed lots of autographs and posed for photos. The Scotties is such an amazing event, because you are treated like a star at every turn. Being on the ice was a different feeling—a bit surreal. I had a highlight reel playing through my head of all the years I had been there, and the many changes to the sport that had happened since my first trip to the event in 1979 in Montreal. I realized that I had been there for all of the baby steps made in the women's game until it evolved into where it is now, and I was honoured.

In the years since my bacterial meningitis scare I was repeatedly asked about my health, but those questions really ramped up at the Scotties. I did an interview with Sean Fitz-Gerald of the *National Post* before the tournament about what had happened back in 2010. People saw the article and some wanted to talk to me about it, because they'd not had a chance to see me in several years. When I had been sick, I had received many cards and flowers from fans wishing me well. Being back at the Scotties allowed people to come up to me and say, "Glad you made it through your rough patch." No one was gladder than I was.

We had really high expectations going into the tournament, but had a tough draw, playing three of the top four teams right off the bat. The reality is that it's hard to play those teams that are playing every weekend on the World Curling Tour for money and trying to earn points to qualify for the Canadian Olympic Curling Trials. We didn't have that kind of game strength behind us, and I'd learned throughout my career the importance of having that pressure every single weekend in order to compete well. We tried, but lost our first four games. To win against Jennifer Jones, Heather Nedohin, or Rachel Homan, you need to be playing them all the time, especially if you want to beat them at the Nationals. You improve by playing the best teams.

It was difficult to recover from our slow start, but we did, winning our next four games. It had been a rocky start, but we were all in the right frame of mind, eager for the next game. Then we faced Rachel Homan's team. I felt like I was playing a younger version of myself from twenty-five years earlier. Rachel was hungry and had a fierce look in her eyes. She's no-nonsense. I chuckled many times on the ice, reflecting on myself and thinking I was playing against a mini-me. I certainly don't have that level of focus anymore, but I know I once did. It was the first time I'd seen that killer intensity from another player, so that was kind of cool. When I was in the Canadian finals in 1980, 1982, and 1984, I was young. The big difference was that I hadn't had a sports psychologist to help me manage my intensity. I would just get mad, hitting my broom on the ground or kicking rocks. No one told me it was inappropriate behaviour. I had two sisters on the team who didn't care if I kicked the rocks, because they knew I'd get over it. Rachel had a coach and a sports psychologist and had been groomed to be great since she was a successful junior. At twenty-three, she was light years ahead of me when I was that age.

We had such a great battle with Rachel's team. It was a close game all the way to the tenth end, when she scored two.

With a final score of 6–5 in Rachel's favour, our run for the championship was almost over. Even though we had two games left to play, we now had five losses, and that is rarely good enough to get into the playoffs. But I have to admit, I was enjoying the experience of being on the ice and not skipping. When I decided to come back and knew I wouldn't be skipping, I wanted to see how other players enjoy curling. That was one of my missions: just to go with the flow and not fight it, enjoy the ride. I always loved curling, but it came with a lot of stress because of the skipping position. It was one of the luckiest curling experiences I had—to be able to go back with a totally different set of parameters where I was able to sit back and watch in a new way. The pressure is immense for the skip, because the final rock is in your hand to win or lose a game, time and time again. It might not happen in the tenth end, but no matter how bad an end looks, a skip can save the situation with the right shot. It's a lot of pressure that I didn't have to endure that year at the Scotties. I just had to make some shots and contribute what I could, and be a supportive teammate. Without that stress, and enjoying the very special crowd, it was a totally different feeling.

We lost to New Brunswick in our next game and ended the round robin with a win over Alberta, but our 5–6 record wasn't good enough to advance to the playoffs. When the round robin ended, a vignette showing our team's career was displayed on the giant video scoreboard, and the crowd stood up and applauded. We had felt the love of the crowd during the entire tournament; they gave us a lot of appreciation. We shed a few tears watching the years roll by on that giant screen. I think the crowd knew they weren't going to see us back again. That moment felt much like the one at the 2005 Scotties. There, we had seen our run of four Canadian titles in a row end; the crowd had acknowledged what we'd done and so had the players on the ice. It was the same heartfelt emotion this time, but in this case the makeup of the team had changed from our championship run. I was playing in a different position and hadn't been to the Scotties in so long. Probably nobody had expected to see me playing again in the Scotties. I think the crowd realized that was unusual and special, but also recognized we'd put a lot of hard work into the game, and not just leading up to this tournament. It had been a cumulative thing. We'd never been the favourites in any tournament. We were just this hard-working unit, a kind of everyman's team, and I think the fans understood that.

Missing out on the playoffs wasn't what we wanted, but as the saying goes, it is what it is. I was almost neutral about the result. I was ecstatic to be back at the Scotties and happy for that opportunity, but I also felt that the whole purpose of playing on the World Curling Tour and trying to make it to the Nationals was to get enough points to qualify for the Pre-Trials, to ultimately get us to the Olympics. I was happy to have gone through the process one more time when I'd never thought it would happen. As Kim says, it wasn't a fairy tale ending, but a happy ending nonetheless.

Rachel Homan went on to win the tournament, becoming the second-youngest skip to win the Scotties; at twenty-three, she only just missed beating my record. That team has an amazing future ahead of them. For me, the Scotties dream is over, but I'm proud to have six Scotties titles. Even just writing that gives me goosebumps. But time does march on.

I KNEW I WOULDN'T be able to play in either the Nova Scotia provincial playdowns or the Seniors playdowns in 2014, because they conflicted with the Olympic Games in Sochi, which I would be covering for CBC. So the 2013 Scotties would be my last hurrah. In Sochi, I worked with Bruce Rainnie, whom I had known for so long and who had been the master of ceremonies at our team's induction into the Nova Scotia Sport Hall of Fame in 2011. Joan McCusker, who played second on Sandra Schmirler's 1998 gold medal–winning Olympic team, and Mike Harris, skip of Canada's team that placed second in the 1998 Games, were also part of CBC's curling coverage.

In Sochi, I had the privilege of watching some amazing curlers. Winnipeg's Jennifer Jones skipped Canada's women's team, which included Kaitlyn Lawes, Jill Officer, and Dawn McEwen. Going into those Olympics, Jennifer had won four Canadian titles (she has five now after winning the 2015 Scotties), three silvers and three bronzes in the Scotties, and a gold and bronze in the World Championships.

Thunder Bay's Brad Jacobs, who won the 2013 Brier and placed second in the Worlds, skipped a team in Sochi that included Ryan Fry and brothers E.J. and Ryan Harnden. The foursome became the first Northern Ontario team to win the Brier since Al "The Iceman" Hackner's in 1985. Jacobs had skipped in the Brier for four consecutive years before winning, and his team became known for its dedication to physical training, something that has become part of the new norm in curling. Brad's team qualified for the Olympic Trials after finishing in the top two in the Pre-Trials.

Both teams won gold medals, the first time Canada curling had done that in the Olympics. Jennifer's team didn't lose a game the entire tournament, while Brad's team started off slowly, losing two of its first three games, but then went undefeated the rest of the way. I marvelled at how strong the

Canadian teams were and how strong the Canadian program is. The way the program works now, with the Canadian Team Ranking System, a team has to be at its best as a group to have any hope of making it to the Olympic Trials, and be even better to win the Olympics. In Sochi, the Canadian teams were a notch better than the representatives from the other countries, and it was obvious. I'd felt that way before, during the Vancouver Olympics, watching Kevin Martin's team as well as Cheryl Bernard's.

Having watched Jennifer's evolution as a curler, it was my opinion that her team was the best ever in the history of Canadian women's curling. I made this remark after her win and she commented on it later. In a story written by Ted Wyman of the *Winnipeg Sun*, Jennifer said, "It's quite surreal to me to have somebody who has won as much as her and somebody that I respect and admire as much as Colleen Jones to say such inspiring comments about myself and our team. I think the [comments are] very flattering and kind of took my breath away because it came from her and some- body that I respect so much … Colleen Jones, the longevity of her career, is unbelievable."

Of course people get better as curlers; we learn more. Just as I learned from Sandra Schmirler, Jennifer may have taken something from the way we trained—even using sports psychologists in the way we did. Everybody learns something from the current champions. Jennifer is a bright gal to begin with, but she's clearly a student of the game who looks at ways she can improve. Every champion thinks, *How do I get better? How do I make sure somebody doesn't catch up to me? How do I stay on top?* She has clearly worked extremely hard, built a team to win, and looks for ways to continually get better. And, amazingly, she somehow does.

I wouldn't have thought Jennifer could improve further from where she had been two years before the Olympics. She placed second in the 2013 Scotties only a few months after coming back from surgery to repair a torn ligament in her right knee and giving birth to her first child. Recovering from knee surgery was probably even harder than recovering from the birth of her daughter, yet she still found a way to dominate and win at the Olympics. Watching her play and win so remarkably well—with the pressure of representing Canada, which is always expected to win—made me appreciate what Jennifer's team had done. In my career, I've had the good fortune and advantage of playing against both Sandra Schmirler's team and Jennifer's, but the bar just keeps being raised in women's curling.

Will I ever try to make it back to the Scotties or the Olympics? Let me say this: It's never, ever, ever over. In my weird brain, there's always tomorrow and always a chance. I am still living in the mind and body of a person who thinks I'm a lot younger and able. In the back of my head, whenever I'm out throwing rocks it's for the Canadian title. I never mess around when I'm on the ice. I don't think I'll ever lose that, even though I'm in my mid-fifties now. But the bottom line is, I've done the work for a long time and I really don't want to do the unbelievable amount of work necessary to stay competitive. We've been there, done that. As well, the thing about curling is it can't be just one person ratcheting it up; all four team members need to buy into that work ethic. That was the great thing about the five Canadian titles we won. We were all on the same page; we all did the work. That's a hard thing to find in curling, where the athletes are juggling jobs and families and have bills to pay. We were lucky to have found each other. For me, lightning struck six times. We were good, and we were lucky.

A lot of people didn't think we could succeed again. It's true that we didn't get to the Olympics, or win the Scotties again in 2013, but I think I proved all the naysayers wrong.

CHAPTER 11
ZACH AND LUKE

Scott and I have always been on the same parenting page. From the moment both Zach and Luke were born, we were in awe of the miracle of having these perfectly wonderful mini humans in our hands and trust. If there is one job you want to get right in your life, it's parenthood. And we loved every minute of parenting.

We never discussed whether we wanted our children to be curlers. We always thought the kids would do whatever they wanted and find their own passions and goals. Zach has no memory of curling, and claims he never tried it, but he did. Luke played in a Canadian Junior Curling Championships, but was never actively involved in a junior program. He just played with me when I was on the ice and eventually worked his way to playing on a really solid team. When the kids were around four or five, we introduced them to some form of physical activity—it didn't matter what—and both took to that *other* ice sport, hockey. We laid down concrete in our backyard and flooded a rink for them out there. I have to confess that I did try to throw my vintage curling rocks on it, but alas, that didn't go well.

I've always thought Zach is the coolest guy on the planet because he's very eclectic in his tastes. He does so many things well and always surprises me with what he can do. He's blessed with a brilliant mind—he's very, very smart—so that gave him a million options. He developed into a good goalie and played for Nova Scotia in the 2003 Canada Winter Games, on a team that included the great Sidney Crosby. Zach was later drafted in the eighth round and 124th overall in the 2003 Quebec Major Junior Hockey League by the Moncton Wildcats after playing for the Halifax McDonalds in the Nova Scotia Major Midget Hockey League. But rather than play in the "Q," as it's known, he chose instead to go to Upper Canada College (UCC) in Toronto for the final two years of high school after receiving a scholarship. He's been an old soul from birth, and it was his decision alone to go the prep school route and keep his U.S. college options open. He wouldn't have been eligible for U.S. college hockey if he'd played Major Junior hockey. I went with him to Moncton, where we could stay for only two days, because after that he would have lost his National Collegiate Athletic Association eligibility. Zach also went to Wilcox, Saskatchewan, to check out the Athol Murray College of Notre Dame, which has a history of developing good hockey players and was also an option. After then visiting UCC, though, he made the decision to go there. At that time, Corey Crawford, who now plays for the Chicago Blackhawks, was the starting goalie for the Wildcats in Moncton. I think Zach figured he would probably sit on the bench as backup goalie in Moncton, because nobody was going to bump Corey Crawford from his spot.

Before Zach made his final decision, we knew he'd be going to Moncton or Toronto, which meant that either way he was leaving home and we had to let him go. You really can't hold your kids back. You're excited that your children get to live their lives and pursue their dreams, and I think I understood that. But it is still difficult. I remember flying with him to Toronto, and on the flight back home I was bumped up to first class because I was crying so hard. As emotional as it is being a mother, you feel good seeing your child being fearless about moving on and starting to write his next chapter. He was extremely determined and focused, and smart about training. While he was playing hockey, he loved it and embraced it.

After finishing school at UCC, Zach played a few games in Springfield, Massachusetts, for the New England Jr. Falcons of the Eastern Junior Hockey League. And then he had an epiphany, realizing that he didn't want to pursue hockey anymore and preferred to study. He eventually went to Dalhousie University and studied law. He's really got a brilliant mind, but maybe all moms say that about their kids. It was funny to see him walk away from hockey, because it had played such a big part in his life to that point. During his studies, Zach worked in the summers as a kayaking guide in Cape Breton in a place called Aspy Bay, which is stunningly beautiful but because it's in the North Atlantic can turn stunningly nasty in a heartbeat. To become a kayaking guide takes a lot of work, yet he did that and also dabbles in being a bicycle mechanic. He's got a really good social conscience and tries to help people and make the world a better place. He's always volunteered at Feed Nova Scotia, a charitable organization that helps to feed hungry people, and also at Help Line, which provides support by listening to and helping callers work through the challenges they are experiencing. My jaw drops when I look at the things he does. I like to make my home a better place and I like to tell nice stories, but Zach has this incredible conscience and brilliant mind—and he really tries to combine both to make things better.

Watching Zach study toward his law degree, I discovered that it is so much work—it's insane. Scott and I have always looked at him and said, "Wow." To graduate from law school with the work he had to do—the studying and the hours—we couldn't have been prouder of him.

He totally surprised me at the graduation ceremony. As he was walking across the stage after they called his name, he made a left turn and grabbed a carnation that was on the stage. I was trying to get a picture along with all the other parents, hoping to get that great photo, and I thought, *That's odd, he's grabbing a flower. I wonder what he's doing?* After he received his degree, he came off the stage, gave me the carnation, and hugged me. I couldn't stop crying and the audience applauded, too. Afterwards, just about every mother came up to me and said, "You have to know how jealous we were that you were the mother who had the son that thought of doing that." That is Zach: always full of surprises. You just don't know what he will do. I definitely didn't see that one coming.

My father worked as a part-time professor of law at Dalhousie, so it was nice to see Zach graduate from the same school where Dad had graduated and taught. My father, who at the time was battling cancer and in the hospital to have his lungs drained, couldn't attend the graduation ceremony, but he was extremely proud of what Zach had accomplished. My father would have loved to have been there, because he was the kind of person who would attend the ceremony every year simply because he remembered all the work that went into getting his own degree. As we left the hospital to attend the ceremony, my father asked us to tell Zach that he wished he could go. My father passed away about a month later.

Zach was a knight in shining armour during my bacterial meningitis. He brought me his world-class fruit smoothies and visited me wearing the infectious disease suit they made him put on. He's always been supportive. During our curling run, for Christmas one year he gave me an ornament of a hockey player with a quote from Napoleon written along the bottom: "Victory belongs to the most persevering." If I were ever to get a tattoo, this is what it would say, because that quote really sums up the story of our team and my own curling philosophy.

LUKE WAS BORN seven years after Zach. He was a bundle of energy and like many younger brothers, constantly tried to keep up with his big brother. He played hockey because Zach played hockey. He played goalie like Zach, too. But when Luke was twelve, he gave up hockey to pursue his passion for tennis. He was so wild about tennis. We had a court across the street from our house and to help burn off some of his crazy energy, I bought a garbage can's worth of balls and would throw them at him for him to whack. I never guessed he would fall in love with the sport. Soon he was at it all the time, and as his game improved it was clear there was not enough competition and structure in his age group near home. There were only eight indoor courts in the area, and it was difficult to get court time. He would work his tail off, get to the Nationals, and be frustrated by his play there. With so few players in Nova Scotia, it was hard to improve. In the summer of 2008, he decided he wanted to move to Ontario by himself to train at Pierre Lamarche's Ace Tennis

Academy in Burlington. It was difficult enough that Zach had gone away for grade twelve, but Luke was only fourteen when he expressed a desire to move and I wasn't ready for him to leave the nest. But Scott and I were in agreement that we would be supportive, believing that each of our boys had to follow his passion.

We didn't think Luke would really want to stay so far away, because he'd miss his friends, school, and life at home, so he and I went on a trial basis to see if it would work. We lived in a beautiful Comfort Inn for about a month, and it became clear he was loving every minute of his new life. So, before I knew what was happening, he and I moved into a two-bedroom apartment and started calling Burlington home while he chased his tennis dream.

Luke loved the routine of training from six to eight in the mornings, going to school, and then training again from four to six in the evenings. It was hard-core and he just loved it. Pierre Lamarche was a terrific coach. He taught Luke so much—not just tennis skills, but also life skills. It wasn't unusual for kids from Nova Scotia to train there, but not too many had their mom come with them! But Luke was happy with everything. It made our relationship even stronger, and we have a beautiful friendship that comes from that time together.

Luckily, the folks at CBC allowed me to broadcast the weather and sports for the national morning show from the Toronto headquarters instead of the Halifax waterfront. So, as has often happened in my life, things worked out easily, almost as if the universe was allowing things to happen. I took the year off from curling and that was a good forced sabbatical from the game, although I still practised at the Burlington Golf and Country Club. It was a weird and wonderful year, because Scott was back in Halifax, Zach was studying in Spain, and Luke and I were living in Burlington. It was an odd arrangement, but it was a fun year. Scott and I look back on that year and wonder how it ever happened.

Training with higher-calibre players helped Luke to figure out how he could be smarter in his day-to-day training. When we returned home and he began training on his own, he was able to make it work. However, he also went back to Ace a couple of times a year for week-long sessions over the next three years. Luke always had a goal of playing tennis at a U.S. college and received multiple scholarship offers from many wonderful schools in the Southern Conference. We let Luke make his own decision, just as we did with Zach, and he chose the University of Tennessee at Chattanooga because he loved the tennis program there and the whole Tennessee vibe.

Again, from a mother's perspective, it's hard to say good-bye to your child when he goes away for university; it's definitely a life marker when they move out and move on and you think, *Oh my God, where did the time go?* But I have to say, Chattanooga is a pretty cool part of the world. Every time we go down there, we love it. It has a very outdoorsy feel; it's very green, lush, and surrounded by hills, with fabulous biking and an incredible river for paddle boating. There are also microbreweries everywhere, and it is full of Civil War history. For Luke, getting the chance to spend four years there is a life-changing experience. The people all have a Southern drawl, and who would have ever thought this kid from Halifax would wind up there? He's studying marketing and communications, and I have no idea and can't even pretend to guess what he might do when he graduates. But I do know that he hosts a show on the university radio station on a volunteer basis, and he sounds pretty good, I think. I know; I'm biased. Maybe the apple doesn't fall far from the tree.

I'M PRETTY SECURE in knowing that both of our sons will wind up on their feet and not compromise on doing what they love. They will never settle for something less than being happy; that's the kind of guys they are. We just hope they let us hang with them. I look at both of them all the time and think that they are awesome kids. If Scott and I had any part in how they wound up, maybe we'll toast one another with a glass of wine—actually, we have done that from time to time. We always made sure they were our priority. Whatever they needed and wherever they wanted to go in life, we wanted to be there to make it happen. And we tried to show them that their lives were limitless, not from a monetary point of view but that you can dream bigger than what you know. While tennis is Luke's priority now, he has a little of the curling bug. He won the Nova Scotia Junior Men's title playing second for Stuart Thompson and they won the bronze medal at the Canadian Juniors. He says when university tennis is over, he'll be back on the ice, and I will be nervously pacing in the stands.

One of the posters on their bedroom wall was the Nike one with Michael Jordan and this quotation: "I've missed more than 9000 shots in my career. I've lost almost 300 games. Twenty-six times, I've been trusted to take the game-winning shot and missed. I've failed over and over and over again in my life. And that is why I succeed."

I think we always tried to make sure when they were growing up that everything was positive and they knew they could be whatever they thought they could be. We were careful not to create parameters or box them into what we thought they should be. That's probably why curling was never on their radar. Our attitude was, "What do you want to do and how do we make that happen?" That sounds a bit "Kumbaya" now that I hear myself saying it, but seeing the fantastic young men that both Zach and Luke have become, I can't argue with the results.

CHAPTER 12
THE CIRCLE OF LIFE

We all know that nothing lasts forever, but when the end comes for someone we love, it's a shock, as if we thought death would never knock on our door. In the summer of 2013, death did knock on the door. Twice. My father passed away on June 27 at age eighty-three after an ongoing battle with cancer, and three weeks later Scott's mother, Ann, passed away at age eighty. They both lived wonderful lives, but I was not prepared for the finality of their passing. We miss them every day.

Throughout the years of his treatment, my father handled his various surgeries and radiation therapy in such a matter-of-fact way; it almost seemed as though fighting cancer was easy for him. I'm not sure if it's a protective thing that parents do instinctively—always acting like everything is going to be all right—but my dad treated cancer like the common cold: a big pain in the butt, but manageable. Watching him battle, we tried to help as much as we could, but he came from a generation where you suck it up and don't complain. I wish I had more of that quality.

It was clear in 2013 that Dad's health was going downhill quickly, and it became our priority. Of the nine children, only three of us live in Halifax—Barb, Monica, and I—so we juggled Dad's doctor appointments, hospital trips, and ambulance rides, and took turns sleeping overnight at his house. My brother, Steve, came up from Toronto several times and Sheila flew in from Grande Prairie, Alberta. We all did what we could and he fought really hard to get better, but it was clear that the end of his life was approaching.

The experience of helping someone to exit life is powerful. Hard, but powerful. Everybody goes through death eventually. I'm sure there are books written on the subject, I just haven't picked them up. The medical community is very good at trying to extend life and keep people alive, but not as good at helping people die peacefully. We were very fortunate to have a wonderful doctor counsel us and steer us toward palliative care when the time was right. It was offered in the hospital and in hospices, but we chose to bring Dad back to his own home for palliative care. He died peacefully at home shortly after, surrounded by family. We like to say that cancer didn't get him, just old age.

Even though we all know death is inevitable, when you watch it gradually happen to someone you love, particularly a parent, it's hard not to take stock of the life that person has given you. The person responsible for you being on the planet has left the earth. And that leaves a huge hole. One second a person is here, and the next they are not. But they have allowed this whole other circle of life to continue, as you have your own children. Certainly, death changes people in a way they don't always expect. I'm a reflective person and I'm always looking at the circle of life—the reason we're here is because of them, our parents. Losing that connection with somebody who was with me all that time—who raised me and gave me a value system—brought all of this to the centre of my attention.

Scott definitely helped me through my emotional struggle. I could start to break down at the slightest thing. Anything could spontaneously trigger tears and sadness. In addition to talking to my family and hubby, I spent a lot of time with a life coach. Talking things through with people helped a lot. When I felt like crumbling, yoga, a long walk, or a bike ride always helped.

Any end of life isn't easy, no matter the age. Many people might say that at eighty-three he'd lived a good, long life. But I saw him fighting for life. When I would take him home after a hospital visit, he would want to get on his treadmill to work out and get stronger, even though he really wasn't healthy enough. Looking at him, I would think he was getting frailer not just by the day, but by the hour, by the minute. But I marvelled at watching him fight so hard to get better. I hope I have the same grit. We tried to bring dignity and peace to the end of his life. I think we did that. At least, I hope we did.

Then, when he died, it was hard to deal with his passing. Harder than I would have ever expected. I'd have epiphanies throughout the grieving process about what's important on life's journey. There's no doubt that my dad's death has been the most difficult emotional storm I've gone through. I'm embarrassed to say that I used to think a big curling game was life-and-death. But when my dad died, I descended into a deep pit that I thought I would never climb out of. I mentioned my spontaneous crying. Hearing a song, seeing someone who looked like him, seeing what looked like his car—a million things could trigger the waterworks.

We gathered for his funeral: all nine of his kids, their spouses, and a whole pile of grandchildren. After the service at suppertime, we went to the beach at Hubbards and to his cottage and did the "Malachi Polar Bear Swim." Dad loved to swim in the ocean, no matter how cold it was. As we dove in, the sky turned blue and the water was calm and warm. I couldn't help but smile. Something much bigger than any of us seemed to be arranging things.

After most of my siblings returned to their homes, Monica, Barb, and I started going through my father's house. There was so much to pack up and sort through. A lifetime of memories in photos, pictures, and clothes. Everything became something I wanted to hold on to, but then I'd realize I couldn't hold on to it all. Like the Warren Zevon song "Keep Me in Your Heart," the important thing when someone dies is to keep thinking of them. You say goodbye, but you can never really let go when it's a parent. They might die, but they don't go too far. My father is still a big part of me, and I'll never lose that. We are all truly connected in the circle of life, and I'll definitely keep him in my heart.

We were all trying to figure this out and accept life without Dad when Scott's mom, Ann, passed away just three weeks later. That added another layer of grief. She had also been in ill health for a couple of years, struggling with arthritis and chronic obstructive pulmonary disease. She lived in Lunenburg, about an hour away, and was admitted to the hospital about a week after my father passed. When she died, I wanted to hibernate. I felt numb. It was a lot of emotional energy to handle.

I think Scott carried most of the burden, making sure I was okay during that entire time. He was grieving, too, but I probably seemed like a complete basket case. I think I was a little more lost than he was. Scott was the pillar, even though he'd lost his mother. Relief came in many different ways, such as Scott and I going for long bicycle rides to burn off energy and take our minds off of our sadness. Shortly after his mother passed away, we did a bike ride of a hundred kilometres from Lunenburg to Halifax. At the end of it, we were too tired to be sad. That was the first of many long bike rides. There is something cathartic about simply hopping on a bike, aiming your gaze at the pavement, and keeping your legs moving in a circle.

It took a solid six months before the cloud of sadness lifted. It wasn't a twenty-four-hours-a-day sadness; I could compartmentalize it when I went to work. Also, I wanted to show Zach and Luke that life goes on, just as my father would have shown me. I'd have to pick myself up, carry on, and resume my life. Death brings quite a shock, because there is so much finality to it that we think we are prepared for (especially with elderly parents), but no one can ever really be ready. Whether there are warning signs or not, the grieving process is a tough road.

Death has taught me that this journey through life—this kind of ride—is very fast. Even if a person makes it to age eighty-three, it's a very short blip. I thought I had learned that after my close call with bacterial meningitis, but we all have a tendency to forget how short life is. Every day, I've got to remember to have gratitude for the life I have and all the precious moments I still have waiting for me. I get to be part of this human experience. This ride does not last forever, so I'll enjoy it while I am on it.

When someone is dying, life seems to move very slowly. It was hard for me to see the value in anything until I properly grieved and got ready to go on again. Even though I went through the healing process, that moment of helping some-one get to the other side changed me. After Dad and Ann passed, Scott and I carried our heavy hearts for a long time.

Even a year after my father started his descent toward death, an ambulance would go by and it would trigger tears. Anniversaries and holidays were hard. Christmas was very hard. You know that person will no longer walk beside you, but you hope you'll one day be able to accept it with an appreciation for the good times and the good memories.

After both deaths, there were a lot of gatherings with Scott's family and mine, so that was comforting. Everyone was experiencing similar feelings and emotions. I will always look back on the summer of 2013 as a summer of grieving. To lose both my dad and Ann in the span of three weeks was overwhelming. It made me truly realize that this is the only chance you get to spend time on earth.

My mother is still alive, but she is in a memory care facility. She was diagnosed with Alzheimer's disease ten years ago, but may have been living with it much longer than that. She once phoned me to come help her because she was at the shopping centre and couldn't find her car. I should have been suspicious then, but I thought, *Everyone drives a maroon car; I won't be able to find it either.* That probably happened fifteen years ago, but she hid her memory issues well. I wonder what she must have been thinking when she couldn't remember what she'd just done. Alzheimer's doesn't simply arrive one day. It's a gradual slide, and I wonder how afraid she was when she started to experience it.

My father would have been the first to recognize her memory loss. He started doing the cooking and all of the chores. He had been totally devoted to her, but when Dad's health issues affected his ability to take care of Mom, he made the decision to put her in a memory care senior home. This was a difficult time for all of us, seeing them separate and watching her try to find her bearings in her new home. I think we all had a lot of guilt over this, mostly feeling like we weren't doing enough. Of course, this is something many families go through as our overall longevity increases. Each of us has our own family to take care of and jobs to go to, but Alzheimer's requires twenty-four-hour care. We're fortunate in that Mom has maintained her cheerful personality in this stage of her life and has adjusted to her new home reasonably well.

Alzheimer's slowly robs a person of their memories. It's a sad disease. No disease is a picnic, but this one is particularly cruel, because when you lose your memories, who are you? I can see my mom struggling with certain things and thinking, *Where am I?* She's living in a very foggy limbo.

But there are still things that make my mother extremely joyful. We take her to high school musicals and play the Irish Tenors, Irish Rovers, and Louis Armstrong. She just loves it. She's at peace when music is being played or when she's singing. While she might not know where she is, she has remained really positive. Each person with Alzheimer's and dementia is different, but Mom doesn't suffer as much as some people with this disease. Some forget how to walk, or eat; some even become violent. And some forget absolutely everything.

She moved into the memory care home just before Dad passed away. When I visit, she doesn't know me right away. But when I tell her, "It's me, Colleen," she lights up. She has no short-term memory, but she is pretty good at recalling life in the 1930s. Sometimes I'll ask her, "Do you remember when you were in Antigonish?" Or I'll play a game with her where I'll pretend we're in Antigonish and ask her, "Do you want to go to Saint Ninian's for mass?" Talking about the old times or relatives sometimes triggers a memory. She won't have many details, but I can tell there's a familiarity and it brings the old mom back for a while.

Everyone living in the dementia wing of a care home is in a pretty bad stage of the illness, but there are definitely different levels. As soon as we put Mom in a home, we made a habit of getting her outside and into the real world, as I like to call it, and I think that has helped her. I'll take her grocery shopping and have her push the cart, and she really loves it. That was a job she did for a long time—getting groceries for nine kids—so if we can bring her back into some of those memories, she transports to a different time.

Usually on a Saturday or Sunday, I'll bring her to my house for the day, and being in the familiar setting, she'll get back to being herself. She'll ask me, "Oh, Colleen, what are you doing?" because she'll recall my name. Or she'll see our cat, Maya, and call it Souza, the name of the cat we had growing up. She used to call my dog, Brutus, by the name of her dog, Duchess. She'll ask me when we're going to see Poppa, her father, and often think I'm her sister. It's hard, but it's also nice when she says a few words to show that, somewhere, a hint of memory survives. The important thing is that she feels surrounded by family and love, which of course she is. I understand what it's like to lose a parent to cancer, and that's a cruel disease. But with Alzheimer's, you lose your parent a little more every day. Sometimes I find myself referring to my mother in the past tense, as if she's already died. Other people who are dealing with parents with Alzheimer's and dementia have told me they catch themselves doing the same thing. It's not an easy disease to watch.

But as my mother always said, "Getting old is not for sissies." That actually is a Bette Davis quote, but another one I believed was an Anne Jones original growing up. But in their eighties, my parents continued to teach me a lot. The biggest lesson is to live life now, because tomorrow isn't promised so you need to enjoy the moment you are in *now*. I took away from observing their lives that simple living looks pretty sweet. They walked a lot, they ate organically, and they somehow raised nine children and never went into debt. They had no digital life, no cellphones. There were probably many things they could have done better; but darn it, they did the best they could with what they were given. As I watched my father die, and continue to watch my mother struggle, and as I think of what I learned about the fragility of life during my experience with bacterial meningitis, I'm reminded of a few things. I have chased a lot of titles and many stories in my life, but the biggest challenge is to figure out how to live a wonderful, loving, stress-free life. In many ways, my parents provided me with a blueprint to which, yes, I've made a lot of amendments; but the core of it was pretty solid.

EPILOGUE

Z ac Brown Band's "No Hurry" is blasting from my Canadian Tire bike speakers attached to my Trek handle-bars. What an appropriate song. Scott is on my tail and we're on another cycling trip, this one through the beautiful Magdalen Islands, near home. We are on a narrow stretch of road with water and sand dunes on both sides. It is spectac-ular. The sky is light blue, the Gulf of St. Lawrence a much darker blue, and the sand dunes are the softest beige. Purple wildflowers line Route 199. I take it all in.

It's on my bike that I have always hit the reset button, and this trip is that chance. I'm a far cry from the legendary Olympian Clara Hughes, but in my wild imagination I am riding as fast as she does. Cycling gives me something that's a little hard to define, but it amounts to peace. Perhaps it's the five hours in the saddle, maybe it's all the fresh air and soaking up nature, or the endorphins from exercise. Whatever it is, I feel rejuvenated.

Life has ebbs and flows. There are ups and downs, much like a bike ride. With each pedal stroke and every inch of pavement, I think about the past, dream of the future, and mostly soak in the present moment amid the splendour of the Gulf of St. Lawrence.

I want to bring things other than curling into my life. I don't want curling to be the be-all and end-all anymore. This feeling happens naturally as you become older and somehow lose that competitive edge, although I'm not sure I will ever lose it completely. I think I'll still have to work on that. Twenty years from now, when I'm out throwing rocks, I'll still be thinking I'm making a shot for the Canadian women's championship. It's still my dream, my DNA. I can't stop that.

Competing has been my spirit and my passion, and I don't know where it really comes from. I fought it for a long time, and now I feel that's just the way I'm built—the way my brain works—and I embrace it. There was a long period when I felt that the drive to be really good at something was a curse. It takes a lot of single-mindedness, and I was so hard on myself. Nothing was ever good enough. Now I realize that's just the way I'm wired, to push myself a little harder. I might not be as good as I was, but that desire and energy is still there every time I step on the ice—that killer instinct and drive to always get a little bit better.

I'm interested in a much quieter, minimalist life now. I go to yoga every day, bike to work, and eat granola. My whole outlook has changed. I think a lot more about what we are all here for, instead of whatever I spent so many years chasing. I'm sure that change happens to anyone who's gone through something life altering, or something that brings clarity about not taking anything for granted. The illnesses and grieving—life takes on new meaning when you realize you might not wake up the next day to take a breath.

We take for granted every breath we take. I think when you have a health scare, it snaps everything into perspective. The realization is not just that we have only a certain amount of time on earth, but also a very important question: What are we doing with that time? Perhaps I shouldn't be so hardwired to win and get better. However, rather than fighting it, I might laugh at it a bit more. I embrace it a bit more, too.

This much I know: I have been lucky. I have two awesome kids; a husband of thirty-plus years who loves me; six Canadian women's curling championships, two World curling crowns, two Canadian Mixed titles, and induction into the Canadian Curling Hall of Fame and the Nova Scotia Sport Hall of Fame; and more than thirty years in broadcasting. I've been very happy to spend twenty-eight of those years with the CBC—or Colleen's Broadcasting Corporation, as I used to tell the kids it was called when they were really little. My partners in crime—Nancy, Kim, Mary-Anne, and Mary Sue—are not just curling sisters but dear friends, and my seven sisters and baby brother are there for me at every turn.

That's not too shabby. And who knows what more I still might add to the list.

COLLEEN BY THE NUMBERS

RECORDS

249
Games played in the Canadian women's curling championship

227
Games skipped in the Canadian women's curling championship

152
Wins as a Canadian women's curling championship participant

140
Wins as a skip

6
Canadian women's titles won

STATS

WORLD CHAMPIONSHIPS WON
2

21
Appearances in the Scotties Tournament of Hearts

CANADIAN JUNIOR CHAMPIONSHIPS

19
GAMES PLAYED

9
GAMES WON

CANADIAN MIXED CHAMPIONSHIPS

7
APPEARANCES

8
TIMES QUALIFIED

2
WINS

NATIONAL MIXED

80
GAMES PLAYED

49
GAMES WON

CANADIAN SENIOR CHAMPIONSHIPS

38
GAMES PLAYED

24
GAMES WON

33 CANADIAN-CHAMPIONSHIP APPEARANCES

386 CHAMPIONSHIP GAMES PLAYED

234 GAMES WON

AFTERWORD

by Perry Lefko

When Robin Wilson, the longtime coordinator for the Scott Tournament of Hearts Canadian Women's Curling Championship, suggested I write a book about Colleen in 2013, it seemed like an excellent idea. I had written numerous stories about Colleen during my many years covering curling for the *Toronto Sun*. Colleen made reporters' jobs easy because after games she provided us with quotes, which were more often quips. As a journalist, she knew we had a job to do, but her animated, buoyant personality provided us with a little something extra, in victory and defeat.

I had written a book about Sandra Schmirler, whose passing in 2000, two years after leading her team to a gold medal at the Olympics, saddened the entire curling world. Colleen's championships teams had been compared to Sandra's, and Colleen had a relationship with Sandra as a fellow curler and subsequent broadcaster. When I approached Sandra about doing a book about her life in 1999, she said: "Do you think anyone would care?" In some ways, Colleen is the same. I don't think she sees herself as anyone special.

She is more comfortable telling the stories of others in her job as a broadcaster than telling her own life story.

We had to stop early into the project following the death of her father and her mother-in-law a month later because Colleen told me she wasn't in the right frame of mind to continue and needed time to mentally and emotionally regroup. But she fought through it, similar to the tenacity she displayed on the ice. Colleen is a true champion.

I learned more about her than simply what I knew about her as a curler. She is a loving wife, mother, daughter, sibling, teammate and broadcaster, and provided great perspective beyond just curling. This is a woman who grinded it out to become the best in the world, and learned many life lessons along the way, specifically about perspective. Whether the subject was her bacterial meningitis, her father's cancer, her mother's dementia, her sons' decisions to leave home to follow their dreams, her championship team's trials and tribulations, and adapting to the ever-changing world of broadcasting, Colleen talked about it with thought, purpose, and candour.

I am thankful to Colleen for letting me tell her story—although in effect she is really the storyteller—and encouraging me to talk to others to help provide background.

The interviews I did with Colleen's husband, Scott, and their two sons, Zach and Luke, were invaluable, along with the input from some of her siblings, including Barb, Maureen, Monica and Sheila.

Thanks also to Kim Kelly, Mary-Anne Arsenault, and Nancy Delahunt, who were Colleen's teammates when the foursome won five national championships and two world championships from 1999–2006, and Ken Bagnell, their "mental" coach. Some other people from Colleen's curling career who helped in the project included Penny LaRocque, Peter Corkum, Kathy Myketyn, and Heather Smith.

Thanks also to some of Colleen's broadcasting colleagues, including Don Duguid, Chuck Bridges, Paul Mennier, Scott Oake, and Mark Bulgutch.

Bob Stewart, Scott Paper Ltd.'s onetime group vice-president of marketing and former chairman and CEO, helped immensely.

Thanks also to Gerry Geurts, Dave Thomas, Warren Hansen, Al Cameron, Monte Mosher, Con Griwkowsky, Paul Wiecek, and Brian McAndrew for their research and background information. If I've missed anyone, it was not intentional.

Thanks to literary agent Brian Wood for bringing this project to Penguin Associate Publisher Nick Garrison, who supported it. Thanks also to Assistant Editor Justin Stoller, who helped shape the manuscript.

A special thank you to Marie Thompson and Blair Meagher for their hospitality and great food in Halifax.

And above all, thanks to my wife, Jane, and children, Ben and Shayna, for their continuing support. They are collectively Team Lefko.

ACKNOWLEDGMENTS

When I was asked to write an acknowledgement, aka a thank you, I thought, "Wow, where do I begin?" There have been so many people who've raised me up, propped me up, and pushed me along.

But let me begin with this book. It was Perry Lefko's idea and I thought it was all a bit pie in the sky, until the wonderful Brian Wood came onboard and brought with him Penguin Random House and suddenly we were steam-rolling along and this book was happening. So thank you to Perry, Brian, and the patient people at Penguin, especially Justin Stoller and Susan Broadhurst, for their careful editing and trying to encourage me to remember more from the early years! Special thanks for giving me breathing room when my father died and I felt I couldn't continue with the project. You gave me the gift of extra time, which really was a precious thing.

To my curling family: Nancy, Kim, Mary-Anne, Mary Sue, Laine and coaches Peter and Ken—what a ride we got to go on together and thanks for always believing in me as I did in you. It's amazing what you can do when you believe.

To the very first Scotties winners back in 1982, my sisters Monica and Barb and Kay Zinck. We didn't even know what we didn't know, but we were rookishly fearless thinking we knew way more than we did! And that rookie belief allowed us to win!

I owe the late Joyce Myers a debt of thanks for her coaching style that was so positively positive. You thought I was great and you thought I could do it; how could I not believe when you believed in me so much? Gerry Peckham, the high performance director from Curling Canada definitely had his imprint all over our team and I thank you for absolutely everything. You provided such wise counsel all the time. I thank you for teaching us so much.

To my CBC family, a massive thank you for allowing me to have broadcasting/reporting experiences that have been so much fun and in so many great places around the world. But, on top of that, the support you gave to my curling career allowed it all to happen.

And lastly to my own family and it's a big one; a million thanks aren't enough. To Scott, you understood my crazy drive and encouraged it. To Zach and Luke, you didn't care if I won or lost and that unconditional love kept the game in perspective and actually allowed me to flourish. I can't believe how much I have learned from each of you. The support each of us got on the home front was the reason we could soar. To my sisters, Roseanne, Barb, Maureen, Sheila, Monica, Jennifer, Stephanie, and my brother Stephen and his wife Anne—wow, so much support and energy through my entire life. I'm so lucky to have such kind siblings. My parents, although never curlers, taught us all how to pick ourselves up and keep moving along, which actually helped a lot in curling!

Everyone has been a piece in my life's puzzle and I know there are so many more people that I could thank because on this journey I'm on, I have learned from so many.

So thank you. I wrote this book in the hope that it finds its way into the hands of somebody like me when I was sixteen. To realize if you have a dream and a few ounces of talent, surround yourself with fellow believers and you too can do more than you thought possible. Thanks for reading!

INDEX

Adams, Shawn, 122
Adder, Michael de, 20
Afaganis, Ernie, 57–58
Aleksic, Shannon, 167
Almond, Kenny, 25
Anderson, Sherry, 136–141
Arsenault, Mary-Anne, 105–115,
  117–119, 120–121, 124–125,
  127–135, 137–149, 150–151,
  153–157, 159–160, 161–166,
  168–169, 201–210, 213, 237
ATV, 93–95, 97

Bagnell, Ken, 49–50, 123–126,
  127–135, 138–140, 142, 144, 147,
  149–150, 154–156, 159–161, 164,
  166–167, 169, 202
Baxter, Jennifer, 203–210
Bernard, Cheryl, 189, 193, 211–212
Bernese Ladies Cup, 200, 205
Betker, Jan, 131
Bidstrup, Lene, 134
Birt, Suzanne, 142–143, 206
Blanchard, Shelley, 46–47
Bodogh, Christine, 55
Bodogh, Marilyn, 55, 144
Bridges, Chuck, 73, 87–88, 90
Brier Canadian Men's Curling
  Championship, The, 40, 41, 62,
  98–99, 102, 173, 182, 195, 199, 211
Bulgutch, Mark, 181
Burtnyk, Kerry, 54

Cameron, Bill, 90
Canada Games Hall of Honour, 11
Canada Summer Games, 57, 191
Canada Winter Games, 47–50, 53,
  55, 191, 216
Canadian Curling Association
  (CCA), 56, 59, 73, 76, 80, 101,
  110, 118, 123, 173–174, 182
Canadian Olympic Curling Trials,
  10, 135–137, 153–154, 159–160,
  167–168, 208
Canadian Women's Curling
  Championship, see Macdonald
  Lassie or see Scotties Tournament
  of Hearts
Canadian Women's Junior Curling
  Championship, 42–44, 55, 111,
  142, 148–149, 215
Canadian Women's Senior
  Curling Championship, 197–198,
  200–201, 210

Carillo, Mary, 188
Catalon, Andrew, 188
Caudle, Cathy, 102
CBC, 1, 10, 11, 12, 17, 20,
  55–56, 57, 97–104, 112, 114, 116,
  119–121, 157, 161, 169, 171, 173,
  175–176, 180–181, 183–186, 191,
  211, 220, 237
Champ, Henry, 90
Chisholm, Colleen, 46–47
CJCH, 73–74, 87–93
Clancy, Joanne, 90
Clarke, Dr. David, 200
Collinsworth, Cris, 188
Comeau, Sandy, 156–157
Commonwealth Games, the, 18,
  96, 190
Comstock, Blisse, 193–195,
  199–200
Connolly, Pat, 90
Corkum, Peter, 115, 147, 169
Costas, Bob, 188
Crosby, Elsie, 80
Crosby, Sidney, 19, 97, 216
Cunningham, Cathy, 143–144, 201
Currie, Wendy, 79, 82–83

Dacey, Mark, 122, 195, 199
Dagg-Jackson, Elaine, 131, 148
Day, Arleen, 67
Delahunt, Nancy, 2, 105–115, 117–
  119, 120–121, 124–125, 127–135,
  137–149, 150–151, 153–157, 159–
  160, 161–166, 168–169, 197–198,
  200–204, 203–210, 213, 237
Dolan, Kim, 102
Doyle, Meredith, 148
Duguid, Betty, 67
Duguid, Don, 57, 99–100, 106,
  173, 188
Dupont, Madeleine, 193
Dryden, Ken, 89–90

Ebersol, Dick, 188

Ferbey, Randy, 81, 148, 160
Fitzgerald, Sean, 207
Fitzner, Karen, 36
Flemming, Paul, 115, 122
Fogarty, Gerry, 90
Folk, Rick, 147
Fotheringham, Allan, 179–180
Fowler, Lois, 149
Fowlie, Heather, 136

Fraser, Sherry, 136
Fry, Ryan, 211

Gallagher, John, 88
Gaudet, Suzanne, see Birt, Suzanne
Gellard, Kim, 109
Gervais, Hec, 56–57
Good, Bill, 100
Goss, Peg, 144
Gowan, Geoff, 90, 99
Gowsell, Paul, 54
Gushue, Brad, 122, 160

Hackner, Al, 77, 211
Hamer, Kate, 168
Hamm, John, 144–145
Hanna, Jenn, 156–158
Harnden, E.J., 211
Harnden, Ryan, 211
Harper, Stephen, 188
Harris, Mike, 182, 211
Harwood, Jennifer, 12
Hiscox, Heather, 90
Högström, Elisabeth, 72
Holland, Amber, 136
Homan, Rachel, 206–208, 210
Hornstein, Rube, 176
Howard, Glenn, 147, 160
Howe, Rick, 90

Iskiw, Beth, 148

Jacobs, Brad, 211
Johnson, Ben, 172–173, 181
Jones, Anne, 22–26, 30–33, 36–37,
  54, 150–151, 230–233
Jones, Barb, 22–26, 30–33, 36, 40–
  41, 45–46, 51–58, 61–62, 64–69,
  70–79, 93, 101–102, 150–151, 155,
  226, 228, 237
Jones, Jennifer (Colleen's sister),
  22–26, 30–33, 36, 40–41, 228, 237
Jones, Jennifer, 133, 138, 144,
  158–159, 161–162, 168, 206, 208,
  211–213
Jones, Jonathan, 20
Jones, Malachi, 22–30, 31–33,
  36–36, 54, 218, 225–230
Jones, Maureen, 22–26, 29, 30–33,
  36, 40–45, 46–47, 228, 237
Jones, Monica, 11, 22–26, 30–33,
  36, 47–48, 55, 61–62, 64–65, 66–
  69, 70–79, 82–83, 93, 101–102,
  155–156, 167, 226, 228, 237

Jones, Roseanne, 22–26, 30–33, 36, 228, 237
Jones, Sheila, 22–26, 30–33, 36, 40–45, 46–47, 226, 228, 237
Jones, Stephanie, 22–26, 30–33, 36, 40, 228, 237
Jones, Stephen, 22–26, 30–33, 36, 226, 228, 237

Kelly, Kim, 105–115, 117–119, 120–121, 124–125, 127–135, 137–149, 150–151, 153–157, 159–160, 161–166, 168–169, 203–210, 213, 237
King, Cathy, 46–47, 109–113, 136, 138, 156–157, 201
Knickle, Margie, 47–49, 55–58
Knowles, Dawn, 73

Lake, Teri, 193–195
Laliberte, Connie, 79–84, 109–111, 121, 133, 144
Laliberte, Corinne, 79
Laliberte, Janet, 79
Lamarche, Pierre, 220
LaRocque, Penny, 50–54, 70, 73
Larouche, Marie-France, 136, 149
Lavigne, Denise, 48, 55
Law, Kelley, 128, 130–132, 136–137, 167–168
Lawes, Kaitlyn, 211
Le May Doan, Catriona, 11
Leonard, John, 62
Lewis, Carl, 172
Lipsit, Jamie, 184–185
Lockhart, Jackie, 141–142
Lukowich, Ed, 102, 145–146

Macdonald Lassie, The, 50–53, 56, 59 see also Scotties Tournament of Hearts
MacKinnon, Mac, 42
Manthorne, Andrea, 185
Manthorne, Warren, 185
Martin, Don, 97
Martin, Kevin, 160, 173, 188, 212
Mattatall, Mary, 167
Mayflower Curling Club, 35–39, 42, 45, 69, 77, 115, 148, 193
McCormick, Debbie, 145–146, 193
McCusker, Joan, 157, 211
McEwen, Dawn, 211
Mead, Joan, 98–100, 103,
Mennier, Paul, 87–88
Middaugh, Sherry, 131, 136, 139, 148–149, 168
Mitchell, Marj, 15, 58–59, 68

Moir, Bob, 171–172
Moore, Linda, 102
Morash, Shirley, 80
More, Chris, 79
Morell, Jim, 11
Mosher, Monty, 11, 164
Mouzar, Jill, 167, 193
Murphy, Steve, 90
Murray, Charmaine, 51–53
Myers, Joyce, 47, 59, 80
Myketyn, Kathy, 42–45
Nedohin, Heather, 115, 206, 208

Nix, Jocelyn, 205
Norberg, Anette, 134–135, 145, 189, 193, 205
Nordby, Dordi, 118, 145, 150–151

Officer, Jill, 211
Olympic Games, 10, 92, 96, 101–102, 135–137, 138, 154, 160–161, 171–174, 180–182, 186–190, 193–196, 202, 211–214

Parsons, Danielle, 195, 199–200
Patterson, Arnie, 77
Peckham, Gerry, 148
Peters, Laine, 115, 118, 125, 135, 148, 164, 168–169
Pezer, Vera, 133, 142, 144
Pinkney, Colleen, 201
Provencal, Darah, 167

Radford, Mary Sue, 125, 148, 161, 169, 237
Rainnie, Bruce, 169, 211
Rankin, Heather, 108
Rebello, Dr. Rosario, 12
Rice, Gail, 91
Ridgway, Michelle, 136
Rose, Dot, 67–69
Rousseau, Guy, 11

Sanders, Pat, 109
Saunders, Ann, 225, 228–230
Saunders, Bruce, 93
Saunders, Kent, 93
Saunders, Luke, 4–5, 7, 12, 22, 27, 83, 95–97, 103, 115, 150–151, 174, 183, 191, 196, 215, 219–222, 228–229, 237
Saunders, Sally, 47–49, 55–58, 197–198, 200–204
Saunders, Scott, 4, 6–7, 22, 27, 44, 85–86, 93, 95–98, 103, 115, 122, 150–151, 181, 183, 196, 201, 215, 218, 220–222, 227–230, 235, 237

Saunders, Zach, 6–8, 22, 27, 29, 95–97, 103, 115, 150–151, 174, 181, 183, 191, 196, 215–222, 228–229, 237
Schmirler, Sandra, 15, 116–117, 121–122, 131, 133, 140, 144, 157, 182, 211–213
Schöpp, Andrea, 193
Schwenker, Ruth, 72
Scotties Tournament of Hearts, 47, 50, 55, 62–64, 79, 98, 100–103, 106, 109–114, 120–121, 127–133, 137–144, 147–150, 154–158, 161–163, 168–169, 182, 194, 201, 205–210, 213, 237–238 see also Macdonald Lassie
Scott, Kelly, 162, 206
Shutt, Brenda, 51–53
Skinner, Julie, 173
Smith, Arthur, 100
Smith, Heather, 148, 193–195, 199–200, 205
Smith, Kay, see Zinck, Kay
Sobey, Marsha, 197–198, 200–204
Sparkes, Lindsay, 53, 62, 73, 82
Stephens, Doris, 184
Stephenson, Marilla, 91
Stewart, Bob, 62
Stoughton, Jeff, 160
Street, Cindy, 111

Taylor, Scott, 147
Thomas, Dave, 163
Thompson, Carol, 66
Thompson, Jim, 103
Thurston, Jill, 161

Vandekerckhove, Patti, 79

Watson, Ken, 41–42
Wheatcroft, Georgina, 167
Wilson, Robin, 62–64, 100
Wittman, Don, 57, 90, 99–100, 106, 172
World Junior Curling Championship, 54
World Women's Curling Championship, 58, 71–77, 87, 103, 105, 116–119, 133–135, 141–142, 145–146, 150–152, 211
Wright, Dave, 90, 95

Zinck, Kay, 61, 64–69, 70–79, 102, 121, 155, 167, 193–194